BIG
IDEAS
OF SCIENCE
REFERENCE LIBRARY

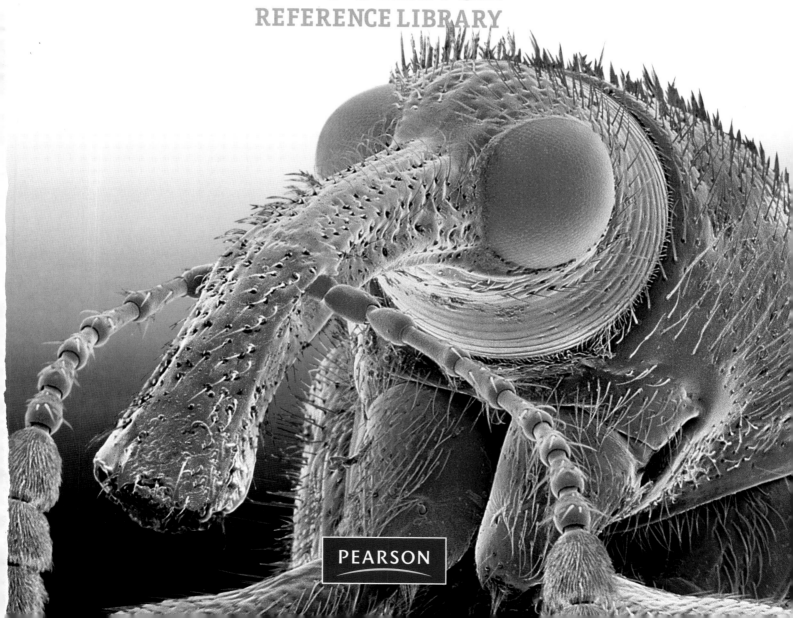

PEARSON

BIG
IDEAS
OF SCIENCE
REFERENCE LIBRARY

Boston, Massachusetts
Chandler, Arizona
Glenview, Illinois
Upper Saddle River, New Jersey

ISBN-13: 978-0-13-369871-8
ISBN-10: 0-13-369871-8

7 8 9 10 V082 14

CONTENTS

KEY
These symbols appear in the top right corner below the topic name
to connect the topic to the branches of science.

 Earth Science   Life Science   Physical Science

BIG IDEAS OF EARTH SCIENCE 🌎

The Big Ideas of earth science help us understand our changing planet, its long history, and its place in the universe. Earth scientists study Earth and the forces that change its surface and interior.

Earth is part of a system of objects that orbit the sun.

Asteroids
Astronomy Myths
Bay of Fundy
Comets
Constellations
Earth
Gravity
Jupiter's Moons
Mars
Mars Rover
Mercury
Meteorites
Moon
Neptune
Pluto
Saturn
Solar Eclipse
Solar Power
Space Probes
Summer Solstice
Uranus
Venus

Earth is 4.6 billion years old and the rock record contains its history.

Atmosphere
Dating Rocks
Deep Sea Vents
Dinosaurs
Eryops
Extinction
Family Tree
Fossils
Geologic Time
Giant Mammals
Ice Age

Earth's land, water, air, and life form a system.

Altitude
Atacama Desert
Atmosphere
Aurora Borealis
Buoys
Doppler Radar
Dust Storms
Earth's Core
Floods
Fog
Gliding
Predicting Hurricanes
Rainbows
Sailing
Snowmaking
Storm Chasing
Thunderstorms
Weather Fronts

Earth is the water planet.

Amazon River
Beaches
Drinking Water
Everglades
Great Lakes
Mid-Ocean Ridge
Niagara Falls
Ocean Currents
Sea Stacks
Surfing
Thermal Imaging
Tsunami
Upwelling
Water

Earth is a continually changing planet.

Acid Rain
Afar Triangle
Caves
Coal

Colorado Plateau
Colorado River
Coral Reefs
Crystals
Dunes
Earthquakes
Equator
Fluorescent Minerals
Geocaching
Geodes
Geysers
Glaciers
Gold Mining
Hoodoos
Ice Age
Islands
Kilauea
Landslides
Lava
Mapping
Marble Quarries
Mid-Ocean Ridge
Mount Everest
Niagara Falls
Rain Forest
Rubies
Sea Stacks
Soil
Terrace Farming
Tour de France
Tsunami

Human activities can change Earth's land, water, air, and life.

Air Pollution
Energy Conservation
Equator
Fuel Cell Cars
Global Warming
Ice Age
Ocean Currents
Rain Forest
Shelter

The universe is very old, very large, and constantly changing.

Big Bang Theory
Black Holes
Constellations
Hubble Space Telescope
Milky Way
Quasars
Universe

Science, technology, and society affect each other.

Astronauts
Hubble Space Telescope
Jetpacks
International Space Station
Mars Rover
Predicting Hurricanes
Robots
Satellite Dish
Science at Work
Space Technology
Space Tourism
Virtual World

Scientists use mathematics in many ways.

Buoys
Doppler Radar
Mars Rover
Measurement
Neptune

Scientists use scientific inquiry to explain the natural world.

Extinction
Predicting Hurricanes
Wind Power
Neptune

BIG IDEAS OF LIFE SCIENCE

Life scientists study organisms, their life processes, and how they interact with one another and their environment. The Big Ideas of life science help us understand how living things are organized, how they get and use energy, and how they reproduce.

Living things grow, change, and reproduce during their lifetimes.

Animal Communication
Bush Baby
Courtship Rituals
Echolocation
Gorillas
Hummingbirds
Hypothalamus
Instinct
Marsupials
Menstrual Cycle
Penguins
Pregnancy
Puberty
Sea Horse
Seals
Sleep
Sloth
Tasmanian Devil
Twins
Worms

Living things are made of cells.

Blood Types
Cactus
Cell Division
Microscopes
Quarks and Leptons
Scent Pollution
Skeletons

Living things are alike yet different.

Adaptations
Aerogels
Bacteria
Bats
Bears
Cactus
Common Cold
DNA Connections
Exoskeleton
Family Tree
Farming
Ferns
Flowers
Frankenfoods
Fungi
Geckos
Giant Mammals
Gila Monster
Insects
Jellyfish
Naming
Patterns in Nature
Plant Tricks
Rain Forest
Red Tide
Redwoods
Scent Pollution
Skeletons
Snakes
Soil
Spiders
Survival
Symmetry
Taco Science
Whales

Living things interact with their environment.

Acid Rain
Air Pollution
Amazon River
Atacama Desert
Bats
Bay of Fundy
Beaches
Biodiversity
Biofuels
Bush Baby
Butterflies
Camouflage
Coal
Colorado Plateau
Deep Sea Vents
Energy Conservation
Everglades
Farming
Forestry
Frozen Zoo
Fuel Cell Cars
Georges Bank

Global Warming
GPS Tracking
Great Lakes
Hybrid Vehicles
Insects
Islands
Kilauea
Light Bulbs
Mid-Ocean Ridge
Mount Everest
Oil Spills
Patterns in Nature
Plant Invasion
Plastic
Population Growth
Rain Forest
Recycling
Red Tide
Renewal
Sea Horse
Seaweed
Seed Bank
Sharks
Shelter
Skywalk

Sloth
Soil
Solar Power
Supercooling Frogs
Sushi
Upwelling
Vultures

Genetic information passes from parents to offspring.

Blood Types
Colorblindness
DNA Evidence
Frankenfoods
Frozen Zoo
Genetic Disorders
Human Genome Project
Hummingbirds
Mutations
Probability

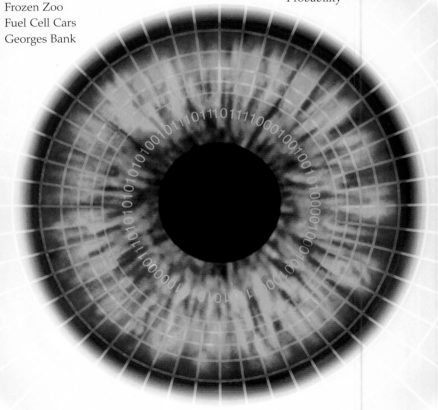

Living things get and use energy.

Algae
Barracuda
Birds
Cell Division
Elephants
Hummingbirds
New Body Parts
Octopus
Scorpion
Sea Horse
Seals
Sour Milk
Tasmanian Devil
Teeth

Structures in living things are related to their functions.

ACL Tear
Aerobic Exercise
ALS
Altitude
Animal Bodies
Birds
Blood Pressure
Blood Types
Brain Power
Broken Bones
Defibrillators
Digestion
Dolphins
Drinking Water
Exoskeleton
Fats

Gliding
Hearing Loss
Heartbeat
Hummingbirds
Jellyfish
Kidney Transplant
Laser Eye Surgery
Left vs. Right Brain
Marsupials
No Smoking
Open-Heart Surgery
Prosthetic Limb
Scent Pollution
Sea Turtles
Simulators
Singing
Skeletons
Skin
Sleep
Sloth
Steroids
Superfoods
Teeth
The Bends
Tour de France
Tweeters and Woofers
Vitamins and Minerals
Weightlifting

Living things change over time.

DNA Connections
Family Tree
Gorillas
Islands
Madagascar
Racehorses

Living things maintain constant conditions inside their bodies.

Allergies
Astronauts
Cancer Treatment
Common Cold
HIV/AIDS
Malaria
Marathon Training
Mold
MRI
Pandemic
Rats
Rheumatoid Arthritis
Scent Pollution
Sleep
Thermal Imaging
Vaccines
Working Body

Scientists use mathematics in many ways.

Census
Estimation
Hazardous Materials
Measurement
Probability
Simulators

Science, technology, and society affect each other.

Biomimetics
Clinical Trials
DNA Evidence
Eye Scan
Human Genome Project
Prosthetic Limb
Robots
Science at Work
Truth in Advertising

Scientists use scientific inquiry to explain the natural world.

BPA
Crittercam
Forensics
Human Genome Project
Naming
Quarks and Leptons
Truth in Advertising

BIG IDEAS OF PHYSICAL SCIENCE

Physical scientists study matter and energy. The Big Ideas of physical science help us describe the objects we see around us and understand their properties, motions, and interactions.

A net force causes an object's motion to change.

Asteroids
Astronauts
Bridges
Collision
Crew
Drag Racing
Formula 1 Car
Gravitron
Gravity
Hockey
Hovercraft
Jetpacks
Meteorites
Quasars
Roller Coaster
Sailing
Skydiving
Snowboard
Tour de France

Energy can take different forms but is always conserved.

Aerogels
ALS
Aurora Borealis
Bicycles
Black Holes
Bridges
Bungee Jumping
Catapults
Cordless Drill
Crew
Defibrillators
Earth's Core
Energy Conservation
Geocaching
Gliding
Headphones
Hoover Dam
Hybrid Vehicles
Lichtenberg Figures
Lifting Electromagnets
Light Bulbs
Microscopes
MP3 Player
MRI
Niagara Falls
Radio
Roller Coaster
Rube Goldberg Devices
Skyscraper
Skywalk
Submarines
Taco Science
Thermal Imaging
Weightlifting

Waves transmit energy.

Animal Communication
Cellphone
Color
Digital Camera
Doppler Radar
Echolocation
Eye Scan
Fluorescent Minerals
Geocaching
GPS Tracking
Guitar
Headphones
Hearing Loss
Holograms
Hubble Space Telescope
Hummingbirds
Laser Eye Surgery
Lighthouse
Microscopes
Mirages
Night Vision Goggles
Predicting Hurricanes
Radio
Rainbows
Rubies
Satellite Dish
Sea Stacks
Seaweed
Singing
Solar Power
Sonic Booms
Surfing
Thunderstorms
Tsunami
Tweeters and Woofers
Virtual World

Atoms are the building blocks of matter.

Acid Rain
Black Holes
Body Protection
Caves
Creating Elements
Crystals
Geckos
Glass

Gold Mining
Mars Rover
Melting Point
Meteorites
Nuclear Medicine
Prosthetic Limb
Quarks and Leptons
Steel
The Bends
Water

Mass and energy are conserved during physical and chemical changes.

Digestion
Earth
Fire Extinguishers
Fireworks
Forestry
Hovercraft
Ice Houses
   Lava
     Melting Point
      Scent Pollution
      Snowmaking
       Supercooling
      Frogs
     The Bends

Scientists use mathematics in many ways.

Buoys
Hazardous Materials
Mars Rover
Measurement
Wind Tunnel

Scientists use scientific inquiry to explain the natural world.

Biomimetics
Forensics
Quarks and Leptons
Wind Power

Science, technology, and society affect each other.

Bridges
Cellphone
Formula 1 Car
Hubble Space
   Telescope
Light Bulbs
Prosthetic Limb
Robots
Science at Work

HYPOTHALAMUS

Near the base of your brain lies a group of specialized cells called the *hypothalamus*. It controls the autonomic nervous system, which regulates breathing, blood pressure, and heart rate. The hypothalamus also releases chemicals that travel to the pituitary gland to stimulate or suppress the release of hormones. Hormones are chemical messengers that regulate and coordinate processes in the body. Pituitary hormones influence growth, sexual development, and metabolism. Parts of the hypothalamus regulate blood sugar levels, sleep cycles, thirst, hunger, 24-hour rhythms, energy levels, and emotions. The hypothalamus also controls body temperature. When the body temperature is too high or too low, the hypothalamus sends out signals to adjust the temperature. If you are too hot, for example, the hypothalamus sends signals that cause the capillaries in your body to expand. Expanded capillaries help your blood cool itself faster and can make your face look flushed.

did you know? ....
IN SPITE OF ALL IT DOES, THE HYPOTHALAMUS IS ABOUT THE SIZE OF AN ALMOND!

THE ENDOCRINE SYSTEM

The endocrine system works with the nervous system to keep the body functioning properly. The body's glands and hormones form the foundation of the endocrine system, which also includes the pituitary, thyroid, parathyroid, pineal, and adrenal glands, and the gonads. The hypothalamus links the two systems. Problems in the endocrine system can lead to diseases and disorders such as diabetes, osteoporosis (decreased bone mass), and growth and development problems.

THE PITUITARY GLAND ▼

Just below the hypothalamus is the pituitary gland, a pea-size gland that controls hormone production. The release of pituitary hormones can be influenced by your emotions or by changes in the season. The hypothalamus senses environmental temperature, daylight patterns, and feelings. It sends this information to the pituitary, which may cause the pituitary to release more or fewer hormones. The pituitary can produce chemicals that elevate mood and reduce feelings of pain.

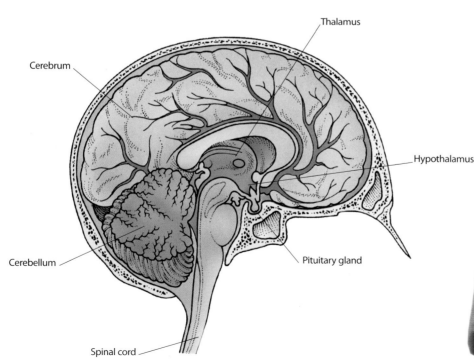

Thalamus

Cerebrum

Hypothalamus

Cerebellum

Pituitary gland

Spinal cord

Bao Xishun, one of the tallest men on record, grew normally until he was 16. Large growth spurts brought him to his present height of 7 feet 8.95 inches (2.36 m) by age 23.

GROWTH SPURT ▲

Puberty-related body development occurs in girls between ages 10 and 14 and boys between ages 12 and 16. The boys above are all 13 or 14 years old. The hypothalamus signals the pituitary gland to release growth hormones. These hormones control sexual development, growth spurts, 24-hour rhythms, and the menstrual cycle.

He Pingping, the shortest man on record at 2 feet 5.37 inches (74.59 cm), suffers from osteogenesis imperfecta, a genetic disorder that causes brittle bones and short stature, among other symptoms.

ICE AGE

Would you believe someone who says we are living in an ice age? You should. Ice ages can last many thousands of years. An ice age consists of both cold periods (glacials), marked by the widespread advance of glaciers, followed by warm periods (interglacials), when glaciers retreat. We are living in an interglacial period. The last glacial period ended about 12,000 years ago during the Pleistocene epoch. In that glacial period, mountain ice caps and sea ice grew. Thick ice sheets extended from the north polar region into Greenland, Russia, and northern Eurasia, and covered Canada and parts of the United States. Ancient ice still exists in Greenland, Antarctica, and some mountain ranges. Scientists study the ice and the grounds where glaciers once were to learn how ice ages affect Earth's climate and geology. Fossilized animals and plant matter, sediment and ice cores, and rock studies all provide evidence of prehistoric life and climate change.

READING AN ICE AGE

Scientists can determine Pleistocene glacial activity by studying rock layers, rock surfaces marked by glacial movement, and boulders carried great distances by advancing ice sheets. There are many fossils from the Pleistocene epoch. Because they are well preserved, scientists can tell exactly when the organisms lived. Fossils of plant pollen, single-celled organisms, and animal remains provide significant data about the effects of climate change on plant and animal life.

Fossilized bone remains

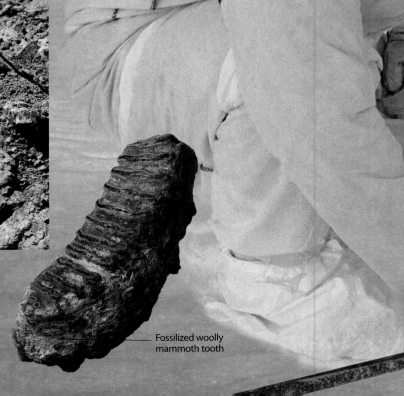

THE WOOLLY MAMMOTH ▲

The woolly mammoth is the best-known fossilized vertebrate animal from the Pleistocene epoch. Carcasses, skeletons, and other fossils have been found in Eurasia and North America. Scientists debate why the species became extinct. Climate change, overhunting, and disease are three strong theories.

Fossilized woolly mammoth tooth

EARTH'S OWN CLIMATE RECORDS

Ancient rocks, dating to about 2.3 billion years ago, contain evidence that a rise in atmospheric oxygen led to the earliest ice age. Sediment tells scientists where glaciers were located. Fossils of pine cones, stems, leaves, and pollen indicate how the movement of glaciers, as well as the climate change it caused, affected where different northern trees grew. Tree rings of fossilized ice age wood show how much growth took place.

Tree ring widths reflect changes in rainfall and temperature from one growing season to the next.

Face masks protect the ice core sample from germs and heat carried by the scientist's breath.

GLACIAL ICE CORE STUDY ▶

Scientists study glacial ice cores to determine how the composition of the atmosphere has changed over time. They extract gases from tiny air bubbles trapped in the core and measure how much carbon dioxide, methane, and other greenhouse gases they contain. They also infer historic temperatures by studying water molecules released when the core melts. Scientists use both sets of data to reconstruct Earth's climate change record.

Ice core sample

Ice core drill bit

did you know? ....

TO STUDY HUNDREDS OF THOUSANDS OF YEARS OF CLIMATE HISTORY, SCIENTISTS HAVE DRILLED ICE CORE SAMPLES DEEPER THAN 2 MILES (3.3 KM)!

ICE HOUSES

Have you ever slept under water? You can sleep under and inside water in its frozen state—in an ice house. An ice house is a building made of ice—water that has been frozen solid. Under normal conditions, water freezes at temperatures below 32°F (0°C). This temperature is water's freezing point, at which the water molecules have lost their energy to the cold air and slowed to the point where they are in a fixed position. Ice kept at temperatures below the freezing point will stay solid. It can be carved into sculptures or cut into bricks. Like igloos, small domes built of bricks cut from packed snow, ice houses protect against chilling winds and extremely cold temperatures.

WELCOME TO THE ICE HOTEL ▼

Jukkasjärvi, Sweden, is the location of the first ice hotel, built of snow and blocks of ice cut from a frozen river. Visitors can experience the thrill of sleeping under an ice roof, drinking out of ice glasses, and enjoying artwork carved out of ice.

did you
know?..............
WATER IS THE ONLY SUBSTANCE WHOSE THREE STATES—SOLID, LIQUID, AND GAS—EXIST UNDER NATURAL CONDITIONS ON EARTH.

◄ A HOTEL THAT MELTS YEARLY

An ice hotel can host guests for only a few months during the winter. In Jukkasjärvi, workers build the hotel in December, and it closes in April when the ice starts to melt. When the air temperature rises above the freezing point of water, the increase in thermal energy in the air causes water molecules in the ice to vibrate. The molecules break free of their fixed positions and can flow as liquid water. Eventually, every piece of ice that makes up the ice hotel melts and becomes part of the nearby river again. The hotel is rebuilt with a different design every year!

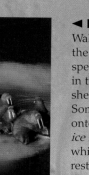

◄ ICY REST STOP

Walruses are large mammals that live in the Arctic—near the North Pole. They spend most of their lives swimming in the frigid waters and hunting for shellfish and other small animals. Sometimes they pull themselves up onto floating chunks of sea ice, called *ice floes*. Ice is less dense than water, which is why it floats, making a nice resting place for a herd of walruses.

INSIDE THE ICE HOTEL ▼

It's common for the outside temperature to get as cold as –22°F (–30°C), but bedrooms in the ice hotel stay between about 17°F and 23°F (–8°C and –5°C). This temperature range is cold enough to keep ice solid, but warm enough for people to be comfortable if they are wearing winter clothes. Visitors wearing warm pajamas sleep in heavy sleeping bags on beds built of ice and snow then covered in animal furs.

Only a fake fire made of ice logs and colorful lights can be built in this fireplace.

Furniture and other structures made of ice stay frozen in the cold rooms of an ice hotel.

INSECTS

With more than 1,000,000 identified species, insects are the most abundant animals on Earth. Scientists estimate that millions more species of insects have yet to be identified. Insects have adapted to jungles, deserts, the arctic tundra, and even hot springs. They are remarkably diverse in their size, appearance, and behavior. Some can swim while others fly. Many jump, play dead, and even sing. Insects range in length from less than a millimeter (fairy fly) to more than a foot (giant walking sticks of Malaysia).

Great eggfly butterfly pupa

Red admiral butterfly

Butterfly eggs

BUTTERFLIES ▶

Butterflies and moths are in the insect order Lepidoptera. Butterflies have four wings covered with colorful scales and a coiled tongue that they use to sip nectar. They inhabit every continent except Antarctica. There are at least 14,000 known species of butterfly and probably thousands more waiting to be discovered.

Swallowtail butterfly

Housefly

Blowfly

Oleander hawk moth

Pink sallow moth

Dragonfly

Cranefly

Maggots

Mottled green moth

Caterpillar

Polyphemus moth

Oak silk moth pupa

Hoverfly

Brimstone moth

MOTHS ▲

Unlike butterflies, moths are mostly nocturnal, and their antennae are feathery rather than club-shaped. There are at least 100,000 known species, the largest of which has a 1-foot (about 30 cm) wingspan! A moth's wings lie flat against its back when at rest; a resting butterfly's wings point straight up.

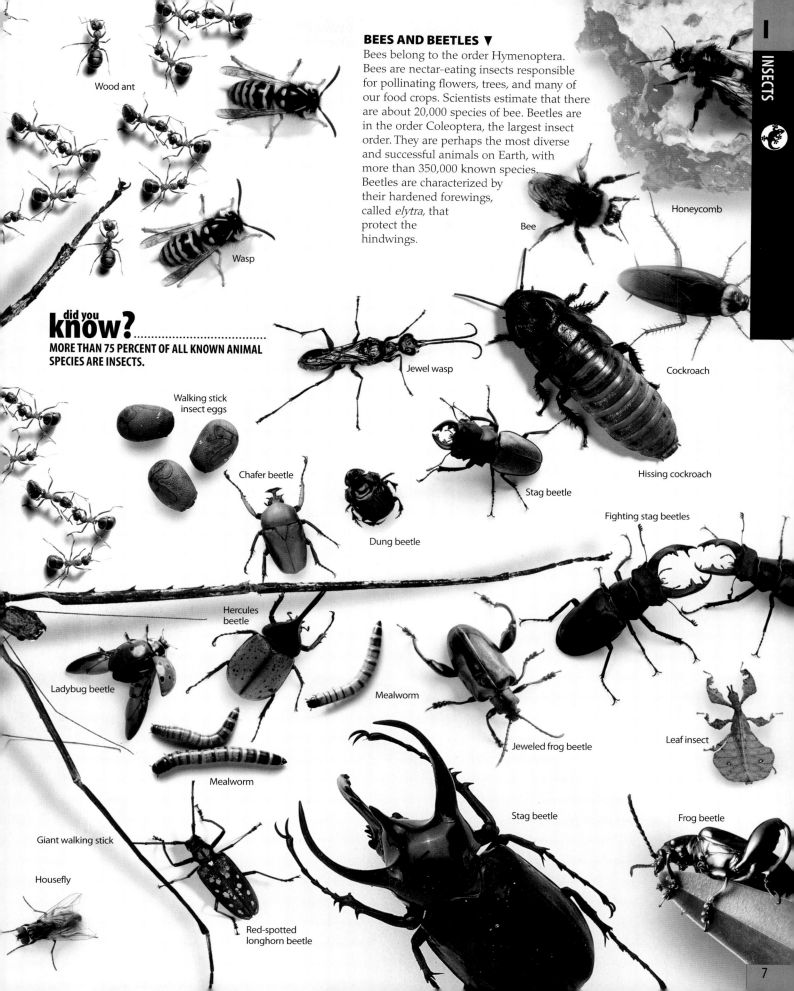

Wood ant

BEES AND BEETLES ▼

Bees belong to the order Hymenoptera. Bees are nectar-eating insects responsible for pollinating flowers, trees, and many of our food crops. Scientists estimate that there are about 20,000 species of bee. Beetles are in the order Coleoptera, the largest insect order. They are perhaps the most diverse and successful animals on Earth, with more than 350,000 known species. Beetles are characterized by their hardened forewings, called *elytra*, that protect the hindwings.

Honeycomb

Bee

Wasp

did you know?

MORE THAN 75 PERCENT OF ALL KNOWN ANIMAL SPECIES ARE INSECTS.

Jewel wasp

Cockroach

Walking stick insect eggs

Chafer beetle

Stag beetle

Hissing cockroach

Dung beetle

Fighting stag beetles

Hercules beetle

Ladybug beetle

Mealworm

Jeweled frog beetle

Leaf insect

Mealworm

Stag beetle

Frog beetle

Giant walking stick

Housefly

Red-spotted longhorn beetle

INSTINCT

How does a spider know how to spin a web, or a mother know how to care for her baby? How does a salmon know how to return to its birthplace to lay its eggs? The answer is instinct. Instinct is a pattern of behavior that animals are born with; it is not learned. Nobody teaches a spider how to spin a web. It is born with this ability. Females of many species, including people, are born with maternal instincts that help them care for their young. Instincts are a key part of the natural world, because they help each species of animal survive and reproduce. Instinct is also one of science's big mysteries. How do these inborn behaviors work?

MOVING WITH THE HERD ▶

This foal, or newborn horse, clambers to its feet within minutes of being born. It will wobble at first, but quickly gain its balance. Then it will follow its instinct to stay close to the other horses. This instinct will help the foal survive. Horses are prey animals that learned long ago to stay in a herd and flee when predators approach.

Depending on its breed, the foal's legs will grow to help it run at speeds of nearly 50 miles per hour (about 80 km/h).

did you know?..
PIGS HAVE AN INSTINCT TO ROOT, OR DIG FOR FOOD WITH THEIR SNOUTS. THEIR ROUND FLAT SNOUTS ARE VERY TOUGH YET FULL OF NERVES.

◀ MATERNAL INSTINCT

Don't get too close. This cow has strong maternal instincts, and she will do whatever it takes to protect her calf. Maternal instinct, the drive that mothers have to protect, feed, and take care of their babies, helps the young of many species survive. If separated from her calf, the mother could become aggressive.

Most instincts are triggered by a stimulus. This calf's suckling instinct was probably triggered by the smell of its mother's milk.

THE HOMING INSTINCT ▼

Sockeye salmon are born in freshwater streams, and then migrate to ocean waters. Years later, they return to their birthplace to reproduce. They may travel thousands of miles to reach their destination! How do they know where to go? Some scientists think the smell of the birthplace stream becomes imprinted on the salmon. Many think that the salmon can sense Earth's magnetic fields. The magnetic fields may help point the salmon in the right direction.

INTERNATIONAL SPACE STATION

In the early 1970s, the United States and Russia were each sending space stations into Earth's orbit. Eventually they decided to join forces to build a space station together. Eleven European countries, Canada, Brazil, and Japan joined in. The result is the International Space Station (ISS)—a laboratory orbiting about 200–250 miles (about 322–402 km) above Earth. Scientists from geologists to doctors to physicists perform experiments in the ISS, many of which have to do with the challenges of living and working in space. Cells, plants, insects, and mice have been studied in order to learn how their reproduction, growth, and health are affected by microgravity conditions.

Canadarm2, a robotic arm to handle large objects and assist astronauts working in space

SPECIAL DELIVERY ▼

Russian Soyuz (shown below), the U.S. Space Shuttle, and European spacecraft can dock at the ISS. They carry astronauts from all cooperating countries to and from the station. Between piloted missions, pilotless delivery vehicles, such as Russian Progress vehicles, also deliver supplies. These vehicles are computer-controlled. They may be programmed to dock with the ISS, or astronauts aboard the ISS can use a robot arm to grab a supply vehicle. While there, supply vehicles use their engine power to help keep the station in its orbit by raising its altitude and controlling its orientation. They also bring the trash back to Earth.

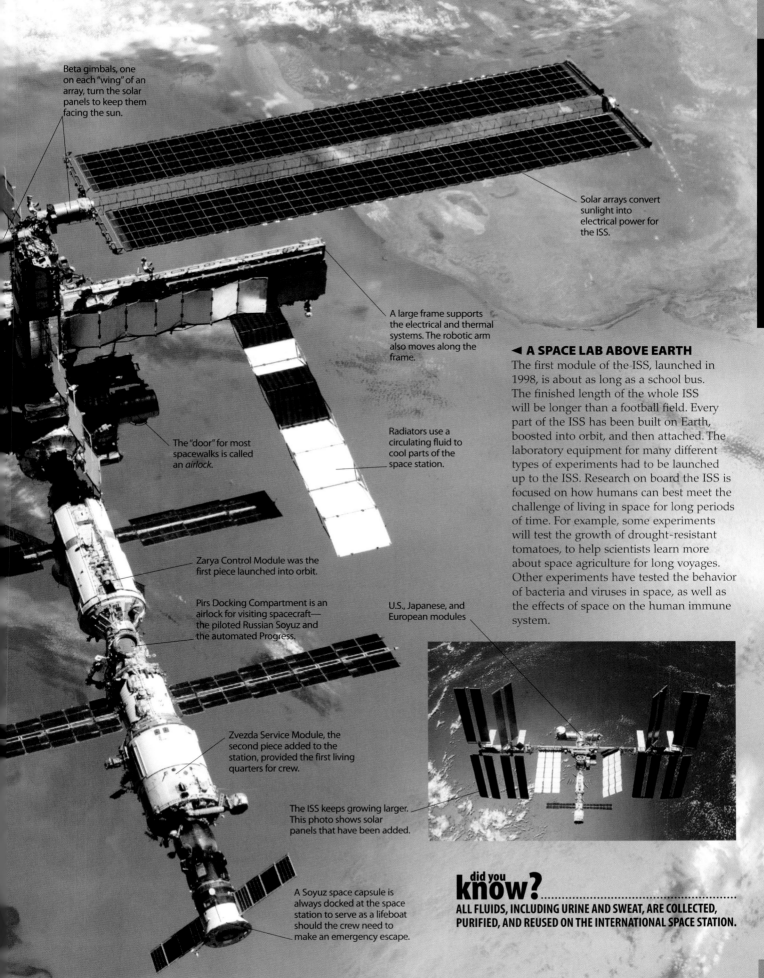

Beta gimbals, one on each "wing" of an array, turn the solar panels to keep them facing the sun.

Solar arrays convert sunlight into electrical power for the ISS.

A large frame supports the electrical and thermal systems. The robotic arm also moves along the frame.

The "door" for most spacewalks is called an *airlock*.

Radiators use a circulating fluid to cool parts of the space station.

Zarya Control Module was the first piece launched into orbit.

Pirs Docking Compartment is an airlock for visiting spacecraft— the piloted Russian Soyuz and the automated Progress.

U.S., Japanese, and European modules

Zvezda Service Module, the second piece added to the station, provided the first living quarters for crew.

The ISS keeps growing larger. This photo shows solar panels that have been added.

A Soyuz space capsule is always docked at the space station to serve as a lifeboat should the crew need to make an emergency escape.

◄ A SPACE LAB ABOVE EARTH

The first module of the ISS, launched in 1998, is about as long as a school bus. The finished length of the whole ISS will be longer than a football field. Every part of the ISS has been built on Earth, boosted into orbit, and then attached. The laboratory equipment for many different types of experiments had to be launched up to the ISS. Research on board the ISS is focused on how humans can best meet the challenge of living in space for long periods of time. For example, some experiments will test the growth of drought-resistant tomatoes, to help scientists learn more about space agriculture for long voyages. Other experiments have tested the behavior of bacteria and viruses in space, as well as the effects of space on the human immune system.

did you know?
ALL FLUIDS, INCLUDING URINE AND SWEAT, ARE COLLECTED, PURIFIED, AND REUSED ON THE INTERNATIONAL SPACE STATION.

ISLANDS

On a globe, Earth's landmasses appear to have water all around them. So, are all landmasses islands? No. Islands are completely surrounded by water—but they are smaller than a continent. They also differ from continents in the way they form. Scientists believe that plate tectonics—the theory stating that fragments of Earth's crust shift or float on Earth's mantle—created the continents. Most islands, however, form in three main ways. Volcanic activity below the ocean floor caused oceanic islands, such as the Hawaiian Islands, to form and rise above sea level. Continental islands, such as Greenland and New Guinea, are parts of continental shelves. They became isolated when glacial ice melted, flooding and covering the land that connected them to the continent. Islands like the Maldives, located off the coast of India, arose from coral reefs. Over time, enough sand and dust accumulated on the reefs to form islands.

Many of the Rock Islands appear mushroom-like. They are made of easily dissolved limestone that is undercut at the waterline.

did you know?.........
KILAUEA, A VOLCANO ON THE ISLAND OF HAWAII, HAS BEEN ERUPTING NEARLY CONTINUOUSLY SINCE 1983.

THE ISLANDS OF PALAU
The Republic of Palau, an archipelago (group of islands) located near the Philippines, includes volcanic, coral, low limestone, and high limestone islands. Some of the islands are a combination of types. The Rock Islands (shown here) and other limestone islands formed when tectonic plates shifted. The shift pushed parts of ancient coral reefs and ocean floor above sea level.

HOW VOLCANIC ISLANDS FORM ▼

Volcanic islands form when oceanic plates collide and the edge of
one plate subducts, or slides under another. The subducted edge
melts, and the magma rises to form an island. Volcanic islands
also form when oceanic plates move across hot spots in Earth's
mantle, a process shown in the diagram below.

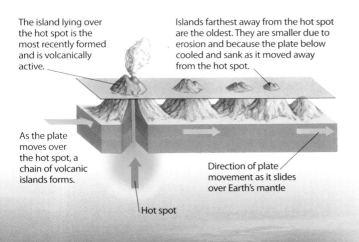

The island lying over
the hot spot is the
most recently formed
and is volcanically
active.

Islands farthest away from the hot spot
are the oldest. They are smaller due to
erosion and because the plate below
cooled and sank as it moved away
from the hot spot.

As the plate
moves over
the hot spot, a
chain of volcanic
islands forms.

Direction of plate
movement as it slides
over Earth's mantle

Hot spot

In the absence of a true
soil layer, vegetation on
the islands grows out of
the loose limestone rock.

▲ THE BIRTH OF AN ISLAND

In 1963, undersea volcanic eruptions heaved up a new island
from the ocean floor about 20 miles (32 km) south of Iceland.
Named Surtsey, this island belongs to a volcanic system of
islands and underwater cones that crosses east central Iceland.

▲ THE FORMATION OF SURTSEY

By the time volcanic eruptions stopped in 1967, Surtsey
was 492 feet (150 m) above sea level and spanned about
1 square mile (almost 3 sq km). The ocean eroded parts
of the island before its core solidified as rock.

▲ THE GREENING OF SURTSEY

The general public cannot visit Surtsey, so plants and
animals are able to colonize there without threat.
Ocean currents, wind, and birds carry seeds and
organisms there. Scientists can study the natural
progression of colonization and observe succession,
the changes in species populations.

JELLYFISH

Are jellyfish really fish made out of jelly? No, but they are more than 95 percent water and have no head, no heart, and no skeleton. These invertebrates are called *cnidarians*, animals that have radial symmetry and take food into their body cavity. Jellyfish are carnivores. They catch their prey by stinging them with hundreds of thousands of tiny poisonous barbs found on the jellyfish's tentacles. Some giant species have trailing tentacles more than 100 feet (about 30 m) long, while some of the most deadly are smaller than your hand! Human influence may be causing increases in some jelly populations. Overfishing has caused jellyfish to thrive. Fish feed on much of the same prey as jellies. Without fish, the jellies are able to move in with less competition for food. In addition, lower levels of oxygen in the ocean due to pollution and climate change favor jellyfish over other species. In recent years, giant blooms of jellies have covered hundreds of square miles, causing damage to the fishing and other ocean industries.

ADRIFT IN THE OCEAN ▶

These creatures have complicated life cycles. The jellies that we usually think of are in the free-swimming medusa, or adult, stage. They drift over long distances, largely at the mercy of the ocean's currents and tides. However, they can move themselves around a little by contracting the muscles at the edge of their bell. Jellies are without a brain or a central nervous system, so a simple set of nerves controls these muscles. These nerves also allow the jelly to detect light and smells, and to stay upright!

3. Water is squeezed out from under the bell, pushing the jellyfish gently along.

2. The jellyfish contracts its marginal bell muscles—much like tightening a drawstring on a bag.

1. The muscles around the edge of the bell are relaxed, ready to contract.

The bell is the "body" of a jellyfish. It is primarily a jellylike substance, sandwiched between protective inner and outer layers.

The "frilly" oral arms are primed with stinging cells to trap prey. There are usually 4 or 8 of these arms surrounding the jelly's mouth.

There is only one opening on a jelly, and this serves as both mouth and anus.

did you know?...

FOUND OFF JAPAN'S COAST, THE GIGANTIC NOMURA JELLYFISH CAN REACH 6.5 FEET (ALMOST 2 M) IN DIAMETER AND WEIGH AS MUCH AS 440 POUNDS (ALMOST 200 KG)!

◄ OUCH!

Not all jellyfish stings harm humans, but most often being brushed by a jelly leads to discomfort—or worse. Most jellies have stinging cells on their tentacles and oral arms. The stinging cells have barbs on them. The cells are stored coiled, then released into prey, where the barbs help them stick. While these poison-tipped stinging cells are intended to catch food for the jelly, they can cause itching, fever, cramping, or even death for humans, too. Stinging sea nettle jellyfish like the ones shown here occur along the east coast of the United States in the summer. They can cause a nasty rash for unlucky swimmers. People on the Australian coast have to be more careful when the Irukandji jelly is around. This transparent, hard-to-spot jelly is tiny, only 1 inch (2.54 cm) across, but its sting can cause death within days.

Many species of jelly have long stinging tentacles trailing behind them, rather like fishing lines.

JETPACKS

In 2008, a man flew 1,500 feet (457 m) without wings across the 1,000-foot-deep (almost 305-m) Royal Gorge in Colorado. It took him 21 seconds, which is lucky, because he had only about 30 seconds' worth of fuel. Stuntman Eric Scott, shown below, pilots what's called a *jetpack*. Technically, he is using a rocket pack, because a rocket—not a jet engine—powers the pack. Both rockets and jets use the force called *thrust* to lift off the ground. Thrust propels a vehicle forward in reaction to the force of gas shooting out the vehicle's tail. But jets and rockets create thrust in different ways. Rockets burn fuel quickly, and are pushed forward by the exhaust. Jet engines burn fuel more slowly, powering turbines that move air through at high speed. Using jet engines to make jetpacks that can stay in the air longer is still in development. Meanwhile, rockets do the work, but most people prefer to call these devices "jetpacks."

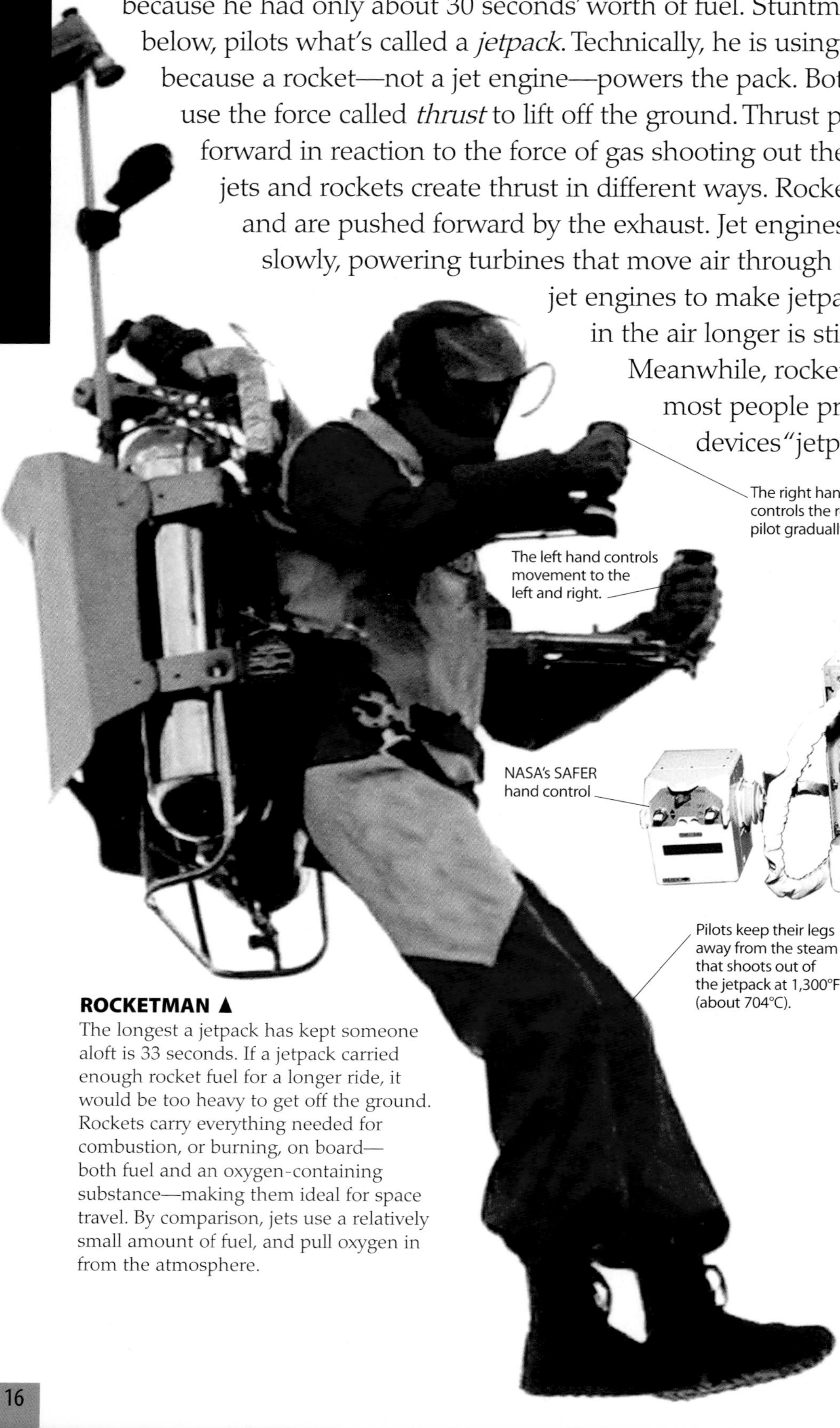

The right hand controls the throttle, which controls the release of fuel. To land, the pilot gradually eases up on the throttle.

Fuel tanks

The left hand controls movement to the left and right.

NASA's SAFER hand control

Pilots keep their legs away from the steam that shoots out of the jetpack at 1,300°F (about 704°C).

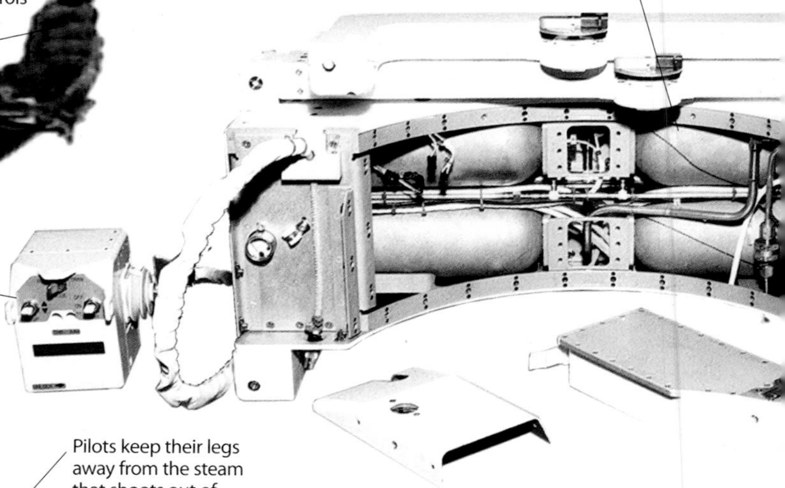

ROCKETMAN ▲

The longest a jetpack has kept someone aloft is 33 seconds. If a jetpack carried enough rocket fuel for a longer ride, it would be too heavy to get off the ground. Rockets carry everything needed for combustion, or burning, on board— both fuel and an oxygen-containing substance—making them ideal for space travel. By comparison, jets use a relatively small amount of fuel, and pull oxygen in from the atmosphere.

MANEUVERING IN SPACE ▲

Working on the International Space Station and the Space Shuttle, astronauts often do construction in space. Astronauts are usually tethered, or tied, to the station during spacewalks, or extravehicular activity (EVA). In addition, they use a **S**implified **A**id **F**or **EVA R**escue, known as SAFER. SAFER straps onto the astronaut's back. Should a tether break, this rocket-powered pack can move the astronaut back to the station at about 10 feet (about 3 m) per second.

◄ UNTETHERED
NASA astronaut Mark Lee tested the SAFER pack while floating untethered outside the Space Shuttle *Discovery*. He used the hand controls to activate the thrusters that propelled him back to the shuttle in hops. He needed only a tiny amount of thrust because at 150 miles (241 km) above Earth, he was experiencing microgravity. SAFER's thrust is created when nitrogen gas burns and the exhaust shoots out of nozzles at high speed.

did you know?..........
IN 2008, SWISS PILOT YVES ROSSY STRAPPED A WING ON HIS BACK, JUMPED FROM AN AIRPLANE, FLEW 22 MILES (35.4 KM) ACROSS THE ENGLISH CHANNEL IN 13 MINUTES, AND LANDED WITH A PARACHUTE. HIS WING WAS POWERED BY FOUR SMALL JET ENGINES.

JUPITER'S MOONS

Jupiter, the largest planet in our solar system, has at least 63 known moons. That is more than any other planet! All but four moons are very tiny—not even a hundredth of the size of Earth's moon. Most of the moons are simply referred to as Jupiter's natural satellites. More than half of them travel in the opposite, or retrograde, direction of the planet's spin. Astronomers believe this motion indicates that these satellites were once asteroids fragmented by collisions and captured by Jupiter's tremendous pull long after its four larger moons were formed. Today, we know more about Jupiter's moons thanks to the information obtained by a NASA spacecraft called *Galileo*. Equipped with many scientific instruments, it orbited Jupiter between 1995 and 2003. During that time, *Galileo* transmitted to Earth thousands of images and readings of the planet and its four largest moons: Ganymede, Callisto, Io, and Europa.

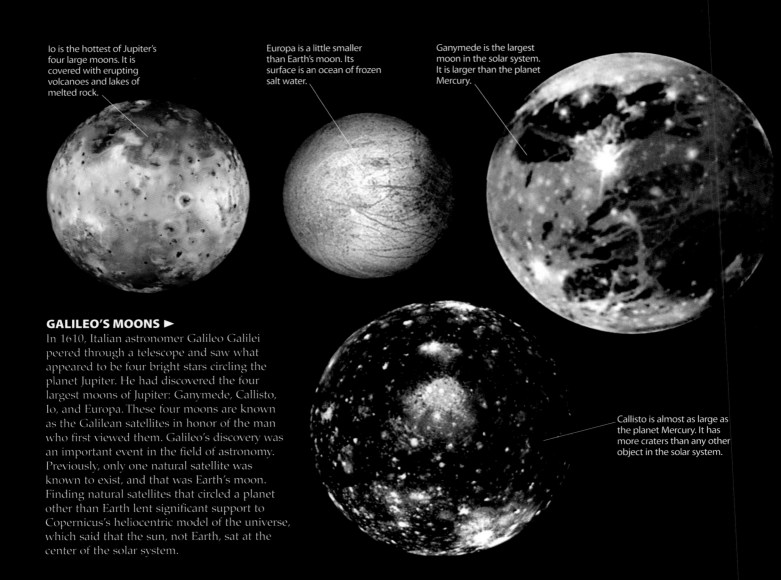

Io is the hottest of Jupiter's four large moons. It is covered with erupting volcanoes and lakes of melted rock.

Europa is a little smaller than Earth's moon. Its surface is an ocean of frozen salt water.

Ganymede is the largest moon in the solar system. It is larger than the planet Mercury.

Callisto is almost as large as the planet Mercury. It has more craters than any other object in the solar system.

GALILEO'S MOONS ▶

In 1610, Italian astronomer Galileo Galilei peered through a telescope and saw what appeared to be four bright stars circling the planet Jupiter. He had discovered the four largest moons of Jupiter: Ganymede, Callisto, Io, and Europa. These four moons are known as the Galilean satellites in honor of the man who first viewed them. Galileo's discovery was an important event in the field of astronomy. Previously, only one natural satellite was known to exist, and that was Earth's moon. Finding natural satellites that circled a planet other than Earth lent significant support to Copernicus's heliocentric model of the universe, which said that the sun, not Earth, sat at the center of the solar system.

Mercury

Earth

Jupiter

Saturn

Uranus

Neptune

Venus

Mars

Sun

Jupiter is the fifth planet from the sun. This image shows the order of the planets and their approximate size relative to one another.

Beneath Jupiter's stormy atmosphere, the pressure is so great that hydrogen gas is compressed to a liquid state.

Ganymede is the solar system's largest moon. It is larger than the planet Mercury.

▲ JUPITER THE GIANT

Jupiter is a giant ball with a gaseous surface, not a solid surface like Earth's. It is so huge that about 1,300 Earths would fill its volume! Jupiter appears to be covered with stripes of different colors. These alternating dark belts and light zones are created by strong winds in the planet's upper atmosphere. Storms rage within these belts and zones.

did you know? IO'S VOLCANIC ACTIVITY IS 100 TIMES GREATER THAN EARTH'S! IT IS THE MOST VOLCANICALLY ACTIVE BODY IN OUR SOLAR SYSTEM.

KIDNEY TRANSPLANT

Kidneys remove wastes from the blood. Without properly functioning kidneys, a body will be sickened by its own wastes. One alternative is a treatment called *dialysis*. Dialysis keeps the body in balance and does many of the tasks of the kidneys. Dialysis treatment can take up to four hours a day, three times a week, and usually is needed for the rest of a person's life. For one method of dialysis, the person is connected to an external machine that filters the wastes and excess water from the blood. The other method filters the blood internally, using a special fluid that is inserted into the abdomen and removed when it has done its job. Another treatment for a failing kidney is a kidney transplant—where a healthy kidney is donated and implanted into a sick person's body. Unfortunately, donated kidneys are in short supply, and it can take years for a suitable kidney to become available for a transplant.

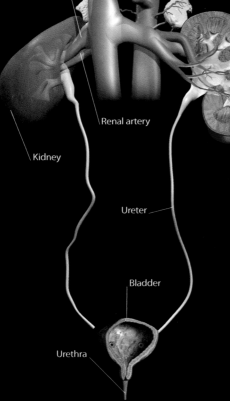

Adrenal gland

Renal vein

Renal artery

Kidney

Ureter

Bladder

Urethra

Vein

Tubule

Artery

Capsule

WORKING HARD ▲

Close to 50 gallons (190 L) of blood pass through the kidneys each day. That's a lot of filtering for these bean-shaped organs, which are only about the size of a computer mouse. Wastes that have been removed from the blood are disposed of as urine, which exits the body through the ureters, bladder, and urethra.

TINY FILTERS ▲

Each kidney is packed with around one million little filtration units called *nephrons,* like the one shown here. In the nephron, blood flows through the capsule, where the waste is removed to the tubules and eventually disposed of as urine.

▼ CHANGING A LIFE

These surgeons are performing a kidney transplant operation.
The complex process takes around three hours. Most often,
the patient's own kidneys are left in place. The donated organ
is inserted into the abdomen and connected into the excretory
system. Transplant organs can come either from a live donor,
often a relative, or from someone who has died. In either case,
it is important for the new kidney to match the blood and
tissue type of the recipient as closely as possible, to lessen
the chances that the body will reject the new kidney.
Rejection happens when the body considers the new
kidney to be an invader, and so the body defends
itself with its immune system. Special drugs help
suppress the body's immune system. These
drugs must be taken for the rest of the
patient's life.

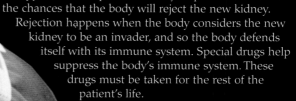

KILAUEA

Kilauea in Hawaii has been active for between 300,000 and 600,000 years, making it one of the most active volcanoes in the world. A volcano does not have to be erupting to be considered active— an active volcano is simply capable of venting lava, ash, vapor, and gases. Kilauea is located on the Pacific plate, one of Earth's tectonic plates. It is situated directly above a hotspot, a column of magma that reaches Earth's crust and forms a vent. Kilauea began as an undersea vent, erupting with lava repeatedly until it emerged from the ocean as an island between 50,000 and 100,000 years ago. Usually volcanoes that form above a hotspot die as the tectonic plate moves away from the column of magma. Most of the islands in the Hawaiian chain are dormant volcanoes that have moved away from the hotspot. Kilauea, however, remains above the hotspot—and active.

Trade winds carry water vapor, carbon dioxide, and sulfur dioxide to the coast, creating volcanic smog, called *vog*, that can affect air quality.

did you know? SINCE 1983, KILAUEA HAS PRODUCED ENOUGH LAVA TO PAVE A ROAD TO THE MOON FIVE TIMES.

KILAUEA'S ERUPTION AREAS

Kilauea erupts from three main areas: a caldera (crater) at the summit and two rift zones (fractures or cracks) located high up the volcano's sides. Lava flows into the caldera and cools, heightening the volcano. Lava that emerges from the rift zones creates ridges that extend outward from the summit. As it flows downhill, the lava cools, gradually building up the volcano's shieldlike form.

The caldera is about 3.7 miles (6 km) across.

Lava that erupts from Kilauea's cone flows through a system of lava tubes (closed channels formed by continuous lava flow) to the sea.

The most recent eruption at Kilauea has been ongoing since January 1983.

PRE-ERUPTION ▲

As magma rises to Earth's surface, tremors, earthquakes, and ground uplift occur in the vicinity of the volcano. Sulfur dioxide gas pressure builds and the summit of Kilauea inflates, like the top of a soda can that has been shaken.

ERUPTION STARTS ▲

The concentration of sulfur dioxide emitted at the summit increases and becomes hazardous to tourist and residential areas downwind. Summit vents exhibit a dull red glow from rising lava, and small streams of lava begin to flow.

ERUPTING ▲

Plumes of lava may rise up to about 1,000 feet (300 m) above the volcano's rim. Usually this lava flows down the volcano's lava tubes. Occasionally explosions at the upper rift zones or summit spew steam, lava, and rock fragments over the surrounding landscape.

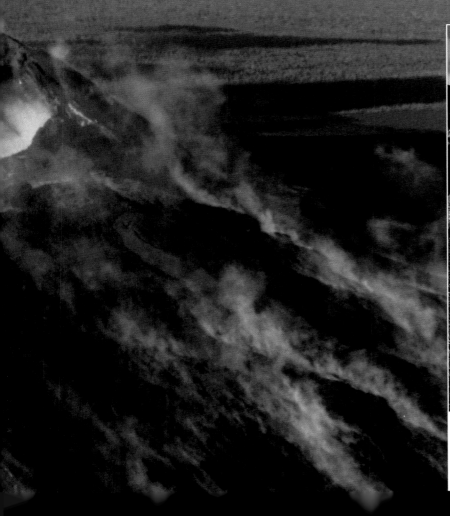

LIFE RETURNS TO LAVA FIELDS ▲

Fern spores and seeds carried by the wind fall into cracks in lava fields. Plants that take root can reach fertile soil below the hardened lava.

LANDSLIDES

Landslides are mass movements of earth, rock, or debris down a slope. They are natural hazards that occur all over the world. Landslides can be small, or so big that you can photograph them from space! Some move slowly—a few inches a year. Others are fast and catastrophic, at speeds of more than 175 miles an hour (about 281 km/h). These mass movements of earth are triggered by natural events such as earthquakes, rainstorms, volcanic activity, or wildfires. They can also be caused by human activities such as road building, flooding, or mining. Landslides can be very destructive. In 1970, a landslide triggered by an earthquake in Peru killed more than 18,000 people and destroyed two towns near Mount Huascarán. They can also reshape the landscape. For example, the huge landslide that accompanied the eruption of Mount St. Helens in the state of Washington in 1980 changed the shape of the mountain and the course of rivers.

did you know?
THE LARGEST LANDSLIDE IN RECENT HISTORY WAS TRIGGERED BY THE 1980 ERUPTION OF MOUNT ST. HELENS IN WASHINGTON STATE. IT WAS 14 MILES LONG (ALMOST 23 KM).

LANDSLIDE IN GUATEMALA ▼
This spectacular landslide occurred in Guatemala in January 2009. Officials believe this landslide was nearly a mile (1.6 km) wide! Millions of pounds of rock, earth, and mud tumbled down a mountainside, burying part of a road and killing at least 33 people. Geologists believe this landslide was triggered by a fault that runs through the area. Faults are cracks in Earth's crust that separate adjacent surfaces, making the surrounding area unstable.

TYPES OF LANDSLIDES ▼
There are many different types of landslides, but all happen when a weakened part of earth separates from a more stable underlying material. Rocks can fall or topple, soil can slide and spread, and mud can flow. For example, soggy soil can weaken and then move downhill or "slump." This image shows how this type of landslide wiped out part of a road in Portugal.

Rock debris buried part of the road.

A pile of rock debris that collects at the bottom of a landslide is called a *talus*.

◄ **SEEN FROM SPACE**

A NASA satellite captured this image of a massive landslide that occurred in China's Chongqing region in 2009. A mountainside collapsed and filled the valley below with 420 million cubic feet (almost 12 million m³) of rocky debris and earth. The landslide buried houses, power lines, and part of an iron ore mine, killing residents and miners.

Debris field

One of the two roads that were partially buried

The very end of the landslide is called the *toe*.

This long, clifflike edge is called a *scarp*; it marks a place from which land broke away.

LASER EYE SURGERY

Each of your eyes has a clear layer on the outside, called the *cornea*, and a lens on the inside under the iris. As light rays enter your eye, both the cornea and the lens bend the rays. For you to see clearly, the light has to focus on the light-sensing area at the back of the eye, called the *retina*. If the light does not focus on the retina, people can change the focus by adding lenses—glasses or contact lenses. It's also possible to correct vision by reshaping one of the body's lenses—the cornea—using laser eye surgery. A laser, which produces one wavelength of light, is focused into an intense beam that can be aimed at a tiny area. With a laser, a doctor can very precisely cut, reshape, or remove tissue. Doctors can use laser surgery not only to correct vision, but also to repair damage, remove diseased tissue, and stop the progress of conditions that can lead to blindness.

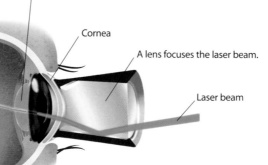

◄ LASER EYE SURGERY
The person having the surgery must be over the age of 18 and have a fairly stable prescription for glasses or contacts. The patient must stay very still, so the head is usually held in a brace. Eye drops numb the eye, and the eye is held open with a device. Corneal laser surgery to correct vision is typically a short procedure, and doesn't require a stay in the hospital. People typically experience very little pain.

Lens

Cornea

A lens focuses the laser beam.

Laser beam

KEEPING THE RETINA INTACT ►
The retina can tear from an eye injury, disease, or aging. It can become detached, meaning it pulls away from the back of the eye. A laser beam can fuse a torn retina back together. For a condition called *diabetic retinopathy*, laser surgery can open a blocked blood vessel, or close a leaky one.

Retina

CORNEA SURGERY ▶

First, the top layer of the cornea is folded back. Then, the laser reshapes the cornea. For nearsightedness, the cornea is flattened. For farsightedness, the cornea is made rounder. This part of the procedure takes about a minute. At the end, the flap is placed over the reshaped cornea, and eventually bonds back in place.

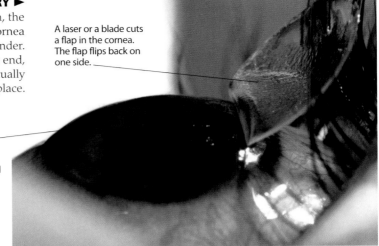

A laser or a blade cuts a flap in the cornea. The flap flips back on one side.

The cornea has no blood vessels. It is about half a millimeter thick and has 5 layers.

did you
know?...................................
SURGERY TO CORRECT VISION COSTS ABOUT $2,000 PER EYE. IT IS CONSIDERED A COSMETIC, RATHER THAN MEDICAL, PROCEDURE.

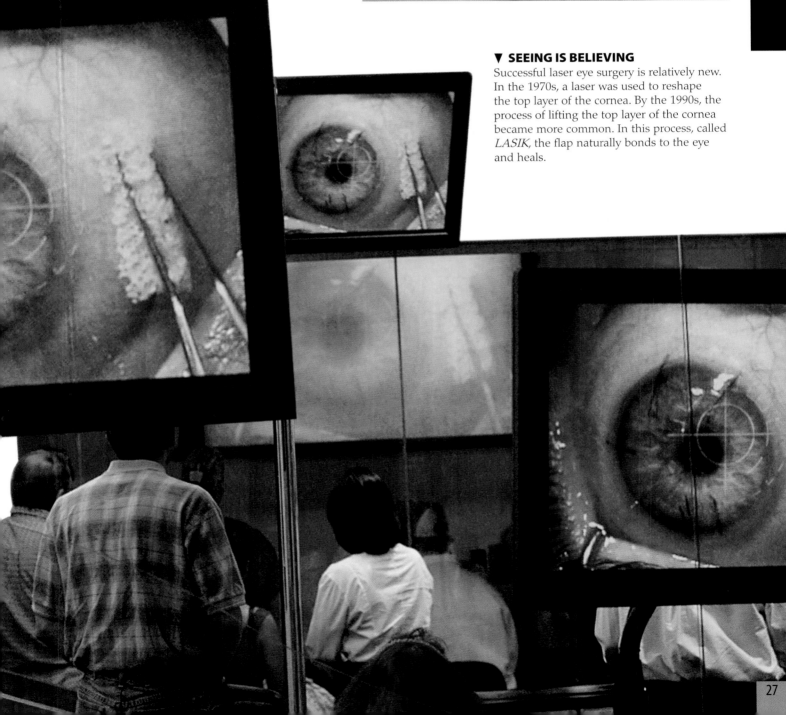

▼ SEEING IS BELIEVING

Successful laser eye surgery is relatively new. In the 1970s, a laser was used to reshape the top layer of the cornea. By the 1990s, the process of lifting the top layer of the cornea became more common. In this process, called *LASIK*, the flap naturally bonds to the eye and heals.

LAVA

While you attend school each day or spend time with your friends, Earth is shifting and changing under your feet. You may not actually feel it, because the movement is so slow. But you hear about it whenever an earthquake or volcanic eruption makes the news. Magma—fiery-hot molten rock—flows beneath Earth's crust. Volcanoes form where intense heat and magma escape to Earth's surface, usually along the edges where tectonic plates meet. Magma that reaches Earth's surface is called *lava*. The temperature and viscosity of magma (how fluid it is) and the amount of dissolved gases in it affect how the lava will erupt. Some lava erupts with a violent explosion, sending rocks, dust, and ash into the air. Other lava forms a lava flow that pours out of a volcano.

Pumice forms when gas-filled, frothy lava explodes from a volcano and hardens. Pumice is a lightweight rock and floats on water.

Pahoehoe lava is smooth, often ropy lava that is common in lava flows.

WHEN LAVA COOLS ▲

As lava cools, it forms volcanic igneous rock, turning black, gray, or dark red. Volcanic igneous rock contains fine crystals and is often glassy. Lava that flows directly into the ocean can cool so fast it shatters into sand. Pillow lava forms when molten lava breaks through the thin wall of an underwater lava tube. The lava squeezes out like toothpaste, creates irregular tonguelike shapes, and quickly hardens.

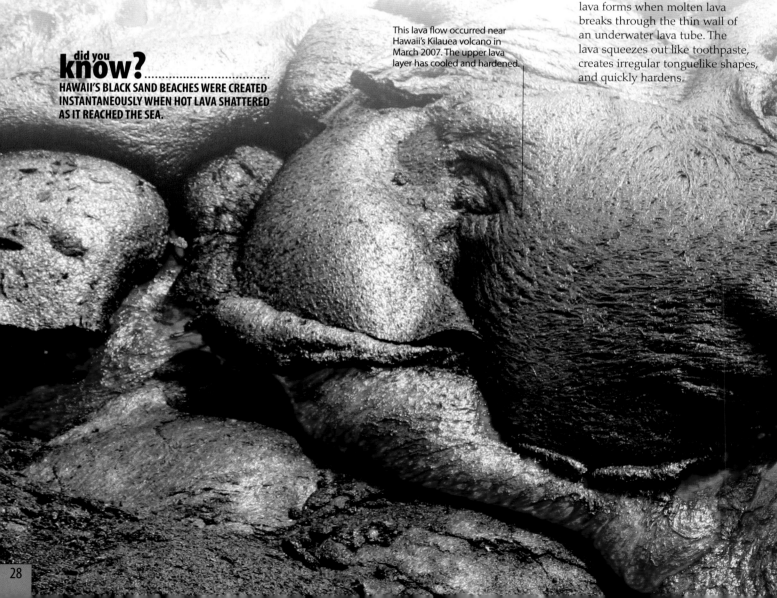

This lava flow occurred near Hawaii's Kilauea volcano in March 2007. The upper lava layer has cooled and hardened.

did you know?

HAWAII'S BLACK SAND BEACHES WERE CREATED INSTANTANEOUSLY WHEN HOT LAVA SHATTERED AS IT REACHED THE SEA.

Lava drips, called *driblets*, can harden into many shapes.

Obsidian is a type of volcanic glass. It is composed of melted sand (the primary ingredient of glass).

LAVA TUBES ▼

Volcanic eruptions can last a long time, creating streams of lava that flow for several hours or days. Ongoing lava streams create flow channels on Earth's surface. When the outer edges of a channel cool and harden, the sides build up. A crust can form over the top of the channel, creating a lava tube. Lava that flows through lava tubes stays hot and fluid much longer than surface lava. When the eruption ends, the lava flows out of the tubes, leaving caves and tunnels, often large enough for people to explore.

LAVA ON THE MOVE ▼

Scientists identify lava types not only by how they erupt but by their silicon, oxygen, iron, and magnesium content. Common lava flows swiftly because it contains less silicon and is therefore thinner than lava that contains high amounts of silicon. Dissolved gases rise easily to the surface of thin lava, so eruptions are not explosive. Dissolved gases cannot easily rise through the silicon of thicker, slower-moving lava. Instead, the gases build up pressure, and when the gas bubbles finally reach the lava's surface, they explode.

The lower layer is still hot and flowing because the crust above helps hold in heat.

LEFT VS. RIGHT BRAIN

Your cerebrum is made up of a left and a right hemisphere. The two hemispheres are connected by a bundle of nerve fibers. The two sides work together to control just about everything you do. Research about the particular capabilities of each side of the brain constantly yields new information. We know that movement of one side of the body is generally controlled by the opposite hemisphere. For example, the left brain controls the right hand. For most people, the right hand is dominant, so their left hemisphere is sometimes considered dominant. The dominant hemisphere is also the usual location for processing language. Almost all right-handed people process language in the left brain. But 60 percent of left-handed and ambidextrous (can use both hands equally well) people also process language in the left brain, with the rest processing in the right brain or in both hemispheres.

The right brain appears to be more involved in processing spatial information and recognizing faces.

STUDY SKILLS ▲
Different study skills tend to use different hemispheres of your brain. Making lists and classifying are considered left brain tasks. Stepping back to see "the big picture" is considered a right brain function.

CALCULATIONS ▲
Scientists think we use the left side of our brains more when we try to solve mathematical equations. The left hemisphere seems to be dominant for math and logic.

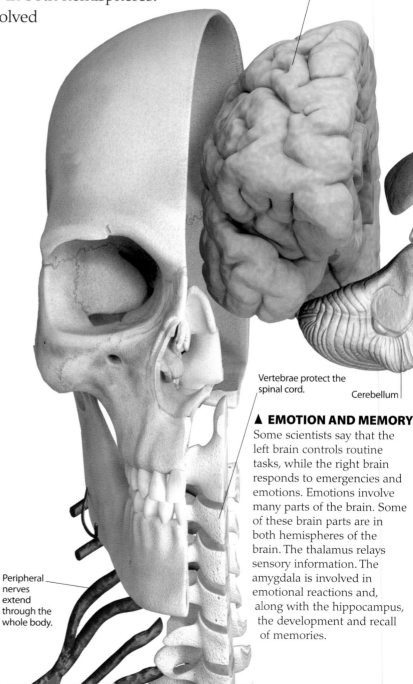

Right hemisphere
of cerebrum

Vertebrae protect the
spinal cord.

Cerebellum

Peripheral
nerves
extend
through the
whole body.

▲ EMOTION AND MEMORY
Some scientists say that the left brain controls routine tasks, while the right brain responds to emergencies and emotions. Emotions involve many parts of the brain. Some of these brain parts are in both hemispheres of the brain. The thalamus relays sensory information. The amygdala is involved in emotional reactions and, along with the hippocampus, the development and recall of memories.

DRAWING A FACE ▲
The right hemisphere of this artist's brain may help in both visualizing the face to be drawn and focusing on developing the many parts of the picture at once.

◄ HEARING MUSIC
Music activates both sides of the brain. The left brain seems to process rapid changes in frequency and intensity. The right side seems to perceive pitch and melody.

did you know?...........................
MUCH OF WHAT WE KNOW ABOUT THE BRAIN HEMISPHERES HAS COME FROM PEOPLE WHOSE SEVERE SEIZURES WERE STOPPED BY SURGICALLY REMOVING THE CONNECTION BETWEEN THE TWO HALVES OF THEIR BRAINS.

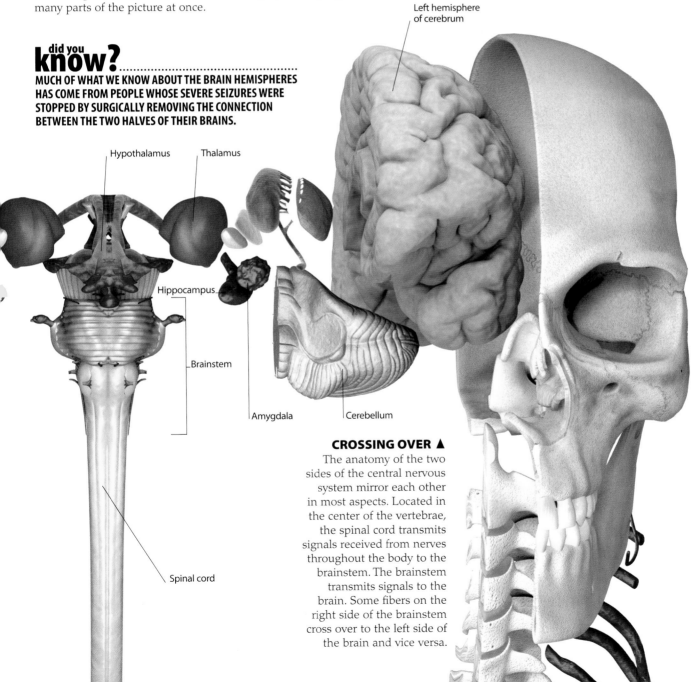

Left hemisphere
of cerebrum

Hypothalamus   Thalamus

Hippocampus

Brainstem

Amygdala   Cerebellum

Spinal cord

CROSSING OVER ▲
The anatomy of the two sides of the central nervous system mirror each other in most aspects. Located in the center of the vertebrae, the spinal cord transmits signals received from nerves throughout the body to the brainstem. The brainstem transmits signals to the brain. Some fibers on the right side of the brainstem cross over to the left side of the brain and vice versa.

LICHTENBERG FIGURES

During a thunderstorm, an electric charge builds up in the clouds and the ground. Suddenly, a flash of lightning pierces the sky in a jagged, branching line. Lightning lasts only a fraction of a second, but there is a way to "capture" the jagged traces of moving electrons in plastic. The Lichtenberg figures shown here were made by building a huge electric potential, called *voltage*, inside a plastic block. When the voltage gets high enough, the electrons move. In less than a millionth of a second, channels form inside the block as the electrons tear apart the chemical bonds of the plastic. The electrons that were trapped in the block rush out through the plastic, releasing the charge. Lichtenberg figures are named after the German physicist who discovered them in the 1700s. When he exposed insulating materials to high voltage, he saw branching images on the surface. Today, we use his discovery in printers and copy machines when charged surfaces pick up toner and put it on paper.

As more electrons are trapped in one place, they repel one another. The greater the electric field, the harder they push.

Conducting paths form when the electrons break apart chemical bonds. Lightning follows a similar path as gas molecules in the air are torn apart.

ELECTRICAL FRACTALS ▶

A fractal is a geometric form in which a pattern is repeated at smaller and smaller scales. This Lichtenberg figure is a good example of a fractal. Look at the widest lines and how they branch. Each smaller branch breaks apart in the same way. Follow the track and you see another branch with similar proportions and angles. There are fractal patterns in nature. Upside down, this figure resembles the branches of a tree.

◀ LIGHTNING IN A CUBE

A particle accelerator pumped high-energy electrons into this plastic block. Because the plastic does not conduct electricity, the electrons were trapped in place, building energy as the electric field grew to millions of volts. Eventually, they had to move. Suddenly, electrons started tearing chemical bonds apart, creating charged channels. With a bang and a flash, electrons rushed away from one another and formed a Lichtenberg figure.

did you know?...............................
LICHTENBERG FIGURES SOMETIMES APPEAR ON THE SKIN OF PEOPLE WHO ARE STRUCK BY LIGHTNING, THOUGH THEY FADE WITHIN DAYS OR HOURS.

Each small branch is a miniature version of the larger branch. As electrons rush apart, they zigzag away from one another.

LIFTING ELECTROMAGNETS

Picking up your little sister's toy truck with a large magnet can make you feel very powerful. Imagine how exciting it would be to pick up a full-size car or a train. To do this, your tool would be an electromagnet. An electromagnet gets its strength from two sources. One source is a solenoid—coiled wire with a current running through it. The other source is ferromagnetic material—material that can become magnetized—such as iron, which forms a core inside the solenoid. The power of these two magnets working together can be hundreds—even thousands—of times greater than a magnet alone. Electromagnets can lift by way of the attraction of opposite poles. They can also lift by using the force of like poles repelling each other, allowing a train to float on air. Electromagnets can do more than lift. For example, they can lock and unlock a car door by turning an electric current on and off. They can move parts of an audio speaker, causing vibrations that produce sound waves.

LIFTING THE MAGLEV ▼

This train in Shanghai, China, is powered by magnetic levitation, called *maglev*. Maglev trains have a magnetic coil that runs along the track, forming what's called a guideway. When a current runs through the magnetic coil in the guideway, it repels a magnet along the bottom of the train, lifting the train about 0.39 to 3.94 inches (1 to 10 cm). Because the train is floating on air, it is not slowed down by friction with the ground.

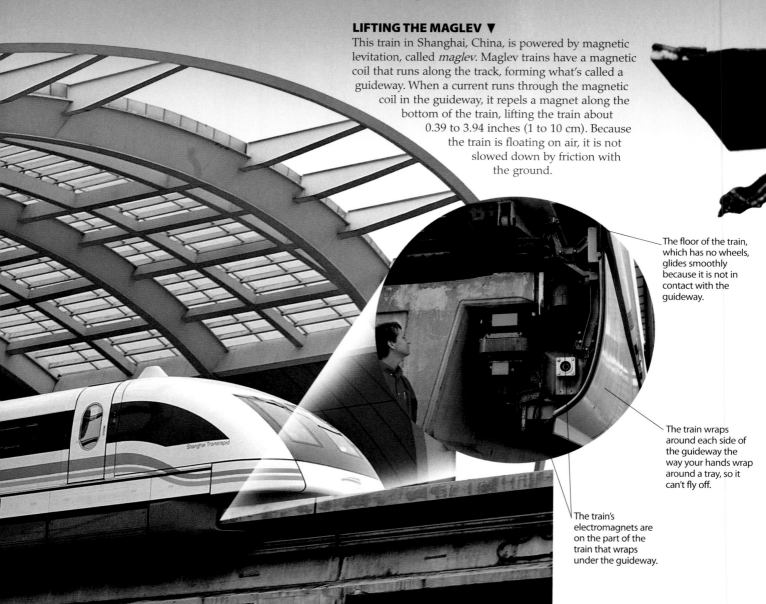

The floor of the train, which has no wheels, glides smoothly because it is not in contact with the guideway.

The train wraps around each side of the guideway the way your hands wrap around a tray, so it can't fly off.

The train's electromagnets are on the part of the train that wraps under the guideway.

Shanghai Transrapid

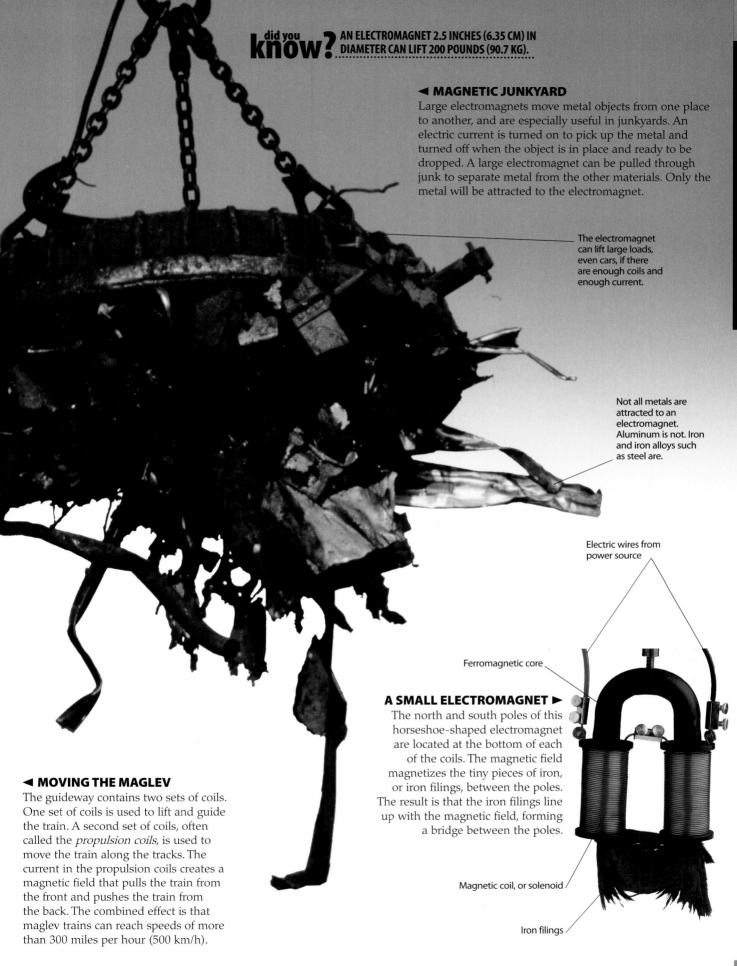

did you know? AN ELECTROMAGNET 2.5 INCHES (6.35 CM) IN DIAMETER CAN LIFT 200 POUNDS (90.7 KG).

◄ MAGNETIC JUNKYARD

Large electromagnets move metal objects from one place to another, and are especially useful in junkyards. An electric current is turned on to pick up the metal and turned off when the object is in place and ready to be dropped. A large electromagnet can be pulled through junk to separate metal from the other materials. Only the metal will be attracted to the electromagnet.

The electromagnet can lift large loads, even cars, if there are enough coils and enough current.

Not all metals are attracted to an electromagnet. Aluminum is not. Iron and iron alloys such as steel are.

Electric wires from power source

Ferromagnetic core

A SMALL ELECTROMAGNET ►

The north and south poles of this horseshoe-shaped electromagnet are located at the bottom of each of the coils. The magnetic field magnetizes the tiny pieces of iron, or iron filings, between the poles. The result is that the iron filings line up with the magnetic field, forming a bridge between the poles.

Magnetic coil, or solenoid

Iron filings

◄ MOVING THE MAGLEV

The guideway contains two sets of coils. One set of coils is used to lift and guide the train. A second set of coils, often called the *propulsion coils,* is used to move the train along the tracks. The current in the propulsion coils creates a magnetic field that pulls the train from the front and pushes the train from the back. The combined effect is that maglev trains can reach speeds of more than 300 miles per hour (500 km/h).

LIGHT BULBS

You walk into a dark room, you flip the switch, and you are no longer in the dark. Light bulbs are amazing devices, but they are so common, you probably don't think about them much. Incandescent light bulbs have not changed much since about 1910. Incandescent bulbs produce light by heating up a wire inside a glass cover. They have been around for so long because they have some real advantages. They light up rapidly, can be made in many sizes, and are inexpensive to make. However, they also have a big disadvantage. To make the thin wire, or filament, glow, it must be heated to between 3,000°F and 4,000°F (1,649°C and 2,204°C). A light bulb uses energy from an electric current, but it converts less than 10 percent of that energy into light, and the rest becomes heat. Because of this, newer, energy-efficient light bulbs, such as compact fluorescent lights and light emitting diodes (LEDs), are becoming more popular. In fact, the United States government is requiring that light bulbs be more efficient. Most countries in Europe have banned incandescent bulbs. Critics of compact fluorescent bulbs complain that the light is too harsh and that the bulbs do not work in some fixtures.

The lights show how urban areas can run together. This example runs from Boston to Washington, D.C. Others show up along the Florida and California coasts.

◄ LIGHTING UP A COUNTRY

How much light do we use? This NASA image captures some of the nighttime light that travels into space from North America. Every major city jumps out as light from homes, businesses, and streetlights streaks away from the planet. About one fifth of all the electricity used in the United States goes to lighting. Increasing light bulb efficiency can save a lot of energy and reduce greenhouse gases.

The inside of the glass contains a thin coating of powder. When an electric current passes through the bulb, it causes the gas inside the bulb to give off ultraviolet rays. When the ultraviolet rays hit the powder, the powder gives off visible light.

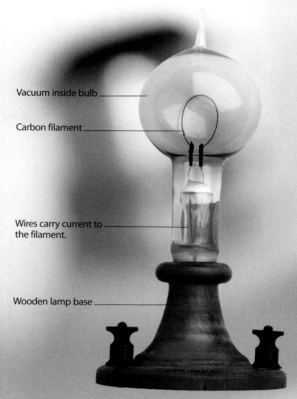

Vacuum inside bulb

Carbon filament

Wires carry current to the filament.

Wooden lamp base

EDISON'S INVENTION ▲

Thomas Edison built the first practical incandescent light bulb. He tried many ideas before finding that a carbon filament could give off enough light. Then he tested different ways to make a good carbon filament. Modern incandescent light bulbs use a tungsten filament instead of carbon, and the bulbs usually contain small amounts of nitrogen and argon gases instead of a vacuum. Other than those changes, the light bulbs in homes today are very much like the design that Edison patented in 1879.

COOL LIGHT ▲

Compact fluorescent lights (CFLs) do not produce as much heat as incandescent bulbs, and they use only about 25 percent of the electricity. CFLs do not heat a wire filament. Instead, electricity running through a tube containing gas produces light. If every home in the United States replaced one incandescent bulb with a CFL, energy use could decrease by 6 billion kilowatt-hours—enough to light 3 million homes.

did you know?
THERE ARE ABOUT 4 BILLION LIGHT BULBS IN USE IN THE UNITED STATES ALONE. MOST OF THEM ARE IN HOMES.

LIGHTHOUSE

You might use a landmark to find your way in an unfamiliar place, but what do you use when you are at sea and there is no land in sight? What do you do at night? A lighthouse can show ships the way or help them steer clear of dangerous coastlines. For centuries, sailors have used lighthouses as highway signs. During the day, their shape and design patterns can be used as a landmark to help sailors steer a ship. At night, they are lit up with powerful lights whose bright beams can be seen for miles, even during a heavy fog. In the past, the light of a lighthouse used to come from an array of candles, a wood- or coal-burning fire, or large oil lanterns. Later, electric light bulbs replaced the flame. Lenses and mirrors are used to focus the light into a long beam so that it can be seen from even farther away.

Just as the keeper closed the door, the wave totally engulfed the round lower portion of the lighthouse.

LA JUMENT LIGHTHOUSE ▶

In the past, lighthouses had keepers—workers who often lived in homes built inside the lighthouse. Keepers made sure that the lighthouse beam stayed lit even during the worst storms. Today, most lighthouse lights are automated and do not require the constant attention of keepers. The lighthouse shown here was completed in 1911 on La Jument rock off the northwest coast of Brittany, France. Many ships travel through these dangerous waters. In December 1989, a moment after this photo was taken, the lighthouse keeper stepped safely inside just before the water washed over the doorway.

did you know?

EACH LIGHTHOUSE FLASHES OR REVOLVES ITS LIGHT IN A UNIQUE PATTERN. SAILORS CAN KNOW WHERE THEY ARE BASED ON THE TIMING OF THE LIGHT PATTERN THEY SEE IN THE DISTANCE.

The brick and concrete tower has an octagonal shape.

The ridges are angled so that they refract, or bend, light.

LIGHTHOUSE LENS ▶

Lighthouses use a powerful lens called a *Fresnel* lens. The lens is made of a central lamp bulb and an outer "shell," forming a transparent lampshade made of hundreds of pieces of cut glass. Some are fixed and others revolve. Revolving lenses produce defined light patterns that are particular to each lighthouse. This allows sailors to locate their position at sea.

MADAGASCAR

Madagascar is a large island country off the southeastern coast of Africa in the Indian Ocean. Madagascar became an island when it separated from mainland Africa about 160 million years ago. Over time, it drifted farther from the mainland to its current distance of 250 miles (about 402 km). This geographical isolation allowed for the development of a distinct ecosystem of diverse habitats including dry and rain forests, deserts, and temperate plains. Many Madagascan species, such as lemurs, are endemic to the island, which means they can't be found anywhere else on Earth! Madagascar's wealth of unique species has encouraged scientists to refer to the island as a "biodiversity hotspot."

The male giraffe weevil's spectacular neck is an adaptation that helps the insect make a nest.

Tomato frogs secrete a toxin from their skin to defend against predators. Their bright red coloration advertises this toxicity and warns off would-be attackers.

Sunset moths fly during the day and have stunning, sunset-colored wings.

DIVERSE WILDLIFE ▶
Madagascar's diversity resulted from the island's lengthy isolation from mainland Africa and from humans, who likely arrived in Madagascar around the year 700. Animals on Madagascar had plenty of time to adapt to new ecological niches and, eventually, evolve into new species.

◀ RING-TAILED LEMUR
One of Madagascar's most recognizable animals, ring-tailed lemurs represent just one of many lemur species, all of which live only in Madagascar and on some small nearby islands. Ring-tailed lemurs, which inhabit the dry forests of southern Madagascar, are opportunistic omnivores, meaning they will eat everything from fruit and leaves to spiders and tree bark.

BAOBAB TREES ▶

Six species of baobabs, or bottle trees, are native to Madagascar. They are often referred to as "upside-down trees" because their strange crowns look more like roots than branches. Baobabs provide shelter and food for many animals, including snakes, squirrels, bush babies, and even humans, who eat the fruit. Their massive trunks are covered in thick, fire-resistant bark and can grow to a diameter of 36 feet (nearly 11 m)!

did you know? ....
ONLY THREE OTHER ISLANDS IN THE WORLD—GREENLAND, NEW GUINEA, AND BORNEO—ARE LARGER THAN MADAGASCAR!

In the rainy season, the trunks of baobab trees expand as they store extra water. When the dry season comes, the baobabs use the stored water to survive.

It may feel like the flu—a high fever, head and muscle aches, tiredness, and chills. But if left untreated, malaria can be a deadly disease. Malaria is caused by a tiny parasite. The parasite infects a particular kind of mosquito. The mosquito carrying the parasite bites humans, transmitting the disease. One way to prevent malaria is by protecting against mosquito bites in areas where the disease occurs. A person who becomes sick with malaria can be treated with prescription medication. The earlier the treatment begins, the more likely the person will recover. With the right medication, people who have malaria can be cured. But, the best way to combat malaria is to prevent it.

◄ SPREADING MALARIA

You cannot get malaria by being near or touching someone who has it. You usually have to be bitten by a mosquito, and not just any mosquito—a female *Anopheles* mosquito. When a mosquito bites a person who has malaria, the mosquito takes in that person's blood and becomes infected. When that same mosquito bites a second person, the mosquito injects a mix of its infected blood and its saliva into that person.

Mosquito eyes have excellent night vision.

Blood is sucked through the proboscis.

did you
know?...............................
BETWEEN 350 AND 500 MILLION CASES OF MALARIA OCCUR IN THE WORLD EACH YEAR, CAUSING OVER ONE MILLION DEATHS.

MALARIA AROUND THE WORLD ►

Malaria is most common in tropical and subtropical areas of the world. Scientists have been working on a malaria vaccine for more than 50 years. The first Phase 3 clinical trial of a malaria vaccine began in May 2009 in seven African countries, with a target date of 2012 for limited public use.

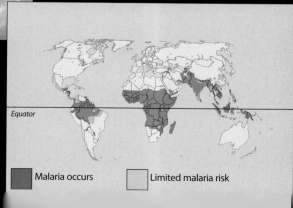

Equator

Malaria occurs   Limited malaria risk

PREVENTING MALARIA ▲

Prevention is the key to stopping the spread
of malaria. One of the most important tools in
this fight is the mosquito net. People living in
or visiting areas where malaria exists should
sleep under mosquito nets, preferably ones
that have been treated with an insecticide.
They should also use insect repellent and wear
long-sleeved clothing when outside at night.

MAPPING

To make sure you can find your way home, you could tie the end of a ball of string to your front door, take it along, and let it unravel wherever you go. This worked for one Greek hero in a maze in Crete, but it's impractical if you really want to explore the world. Instead, people create maps. They record the places they have been, using various ways of indicating a starting point, turns, landmarks, distances, and destinations. Over time, people have navigated by locating themselves in relation to stars, or by sailing along a coast, or by using a map and compass. Now you can find your way to the nearest pizza shop using GPS (Global Positioning System) or mapping software on a cellphone. Or, using Google Earth™, you can zoom to Naples, Italy, and find the pizza shops there. You won't have to worry about getting home, but you'll still be hungry at the end of the journey.

MAP PROJECTIONS ▼

The most familiar map projection is probably the Mercator projection, which unwraps the globe and stretches the wrapping onto a flat surface. Mercator is a cylindrical projection, so landmasses closer to the poles look wider than they are. All projections distort the sphere, but in different ways.

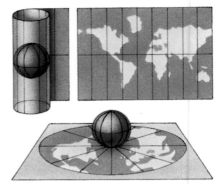

Cylindrical projections make all the lines of longitude appear parallel. On the globe, these lines converge and become very close together at the poles.

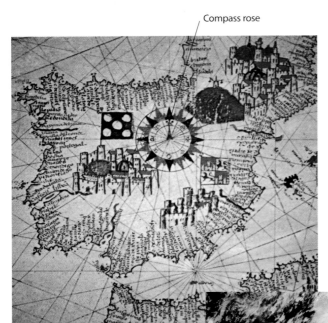

Compass rose

◄ SPAIN 1492

For his voyage across the Atlantic in 1492, Christopher Columbus set out from the coastal town of Palos de la Frontera, Spain. This map, from the town's museum, shows what a sailor of the time needed to know: the ports of Spain, Portugal, and Morocco. A compass rose shows where north is on the map.

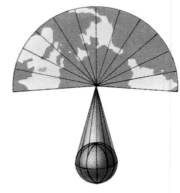

Azimuthal, or zenithal, projections show Earth as if a piece of paper touched the sphere at one point, such as the North Pole. In this case, the edges of the map are distorted.

Conical projections are most accurate at a particular line of latitude or between two lines that the mapmaker chooses to focus on.

SPAIN 2003 ►

NASA satellite maps can show specific moments in time. Comparing images taken at different times can show changes in landforms. Here, annual flooding of a river in Spain shows up as light blue pools in nearby marshlands at the lower left. These marshlands used to be a bay, but eventually the river carried sand into the bay and blocked some of the river's flow.

A map projection of Earth's surface cut into segments along lines of longitude would get rid of some distortion. It also would be hard to read.

TRUE NORTH OR MAGNETIC NORTH? ►

Where is north exactly? Surprisingly, north on a map is usually not the same as north on a compass. The north symbol that you usually find on maps points to what is called *true north,* which is the axis point at the North Pole around which Earth rotates. All of the longitude lines on a map intersect at true north. The arrow inside a compass always points to what is called *magnetic north.* That's because the compass lines up with Earth's magnetic field. Earth is like a big magnet, with a north magnetic pole and south magnetic pole.

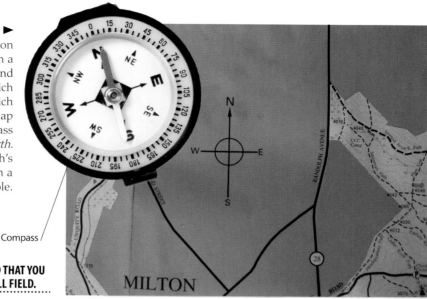

Compass

did you know? SATELLITE IMAGES ARE SO DETAILED THAT YOU CAN SEE HOME PLATE ON A BASEBALL FIELD.

Google Earth's car camera photographs street views.

▲ LOOKING DOWN ON EARTH

Ever since the Soviet Union sent Sputnik, the first satellite, into orbit in 1957, the race to see Earth from above has been on. U.S. satellites soon photographed Soviet missiles from space. Meanwhile, Canadian geographers created the first geographic information system (GIS), a type of mapping software that can analyze vast databases of spatial information, including satellite images. Since then, technology developed in many parts of the world has come together to produce incredibly clear satellite photos of Earth and sophisticated mapping programs. Now, both government and commercial satellites constantly circle Earth and send back photos. That's why you can type your address into Google Earth and see your house from space!

MARATHON TRAINING

A marathon is a grueling 26.2-mile (about 42-km) race. If you are in reasonable shape, you can train to run a marathon in about 16 weeks. By running longer distances each week, you slowly make your muscles stronger. Since the heart muscle pushes oxygen-rich blood through the body, a stronger heart means the body gets more oxygen. During a race, a runner's heart rate increases, and body temperature rises. The body sweats, which cools the body down. For about the first 20 miles of a marathon, runners' muscles are fueled by stored carbohydrates. After this distance, some runners may "hit the wall." This means their stored energy is used up, and the body needs to burn fat for fuel. Burning fat is difficult. During the last miles of a race, a runner might feel faint, have muscle cramps, or find breathing difficult.

◄ WATCH THOSE FLUIDS!

Not long ago, runners were advised to stay ahead of their thirst when they ran marathons to avoid dehydration. Now, scientists know that drinking either too little water or too much water can be bad. Drinking too much water causes the sodium (salt) concentration in the blood to become too low, and runners can get very sick. Many trainers say that not losing a small amount of weight during a marathon may mean a runner has taken in too much water.

THE WORLD'S BEST RUNNERS ►

Some of the best marathon runners in the world are from East Africa. For years, scientists have tried to figure out why this is so. Some evidence points to the fact that many East Africans run long distances to and from school as children. Also, East Africa is at a high altitude. Training at high altitude has been shown to improve performances for endurance athletes.

BLISTERS, BLISTERS, BLISTERS! ▶
Running a marathon is hard on all parts of the body. Feet can rub in shoes to give runners blisters. As they race, runners can become overheated, dehydrated, or overhydrated. Their muscles and joints can become sore or injured. After they finish, runners can become chilled or blood can pool in their legs as their heart slows down.

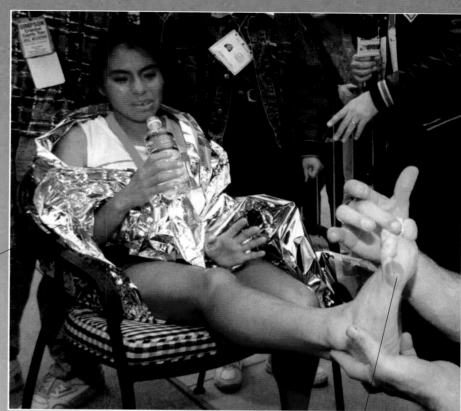

After a marathon is finished, runners are often given Mylar blankets, called *space blankets*, to reflect heat back to their body.

did you **know?** ONLY ABOUT 1 PERCENT OF THE PEOPLE IN THE WORLD HAVE COMPLETED A MARATHON.

Runners are often not aware that they have formed blisters until they stop running. Despite this blister, Lucía Rendón of Mexico finished second in a Los Angeles marathon.

Ethiopian marathoners, led by their British trainer, run along the Mumbai waterfront in preparation for a race.

MARBLE QUARRIES

It makes up the bone-colored bricks in the dome of the Taj Mahal. It gives Michelangelo's statue *David* its smooth, skinlike texture. Even a few toy marbles were made out of—you guessed it—marble! Whether part of an ancient work of art or a kitchen countertop, marble must first come out of the ground— at a marble quarry. A quarry is an open pit where stoneworkers cut rock out of the walls. Different quarries all over the world produce different colors and qualities of marble. Marble forms from a chalky rock—limestone. Limestone forms when sediment that is deposited in layers hardens. Limestone is dull, while marble has tiny crystals and can be polished. How does one type of rock turn into another? This process, called *metamorphism*, is a little like pressing with a spatula on a grilled cheese sandwich in a frying pan. Underground, heat and pressure cause melting and chemical changes in rocks that cannot be undone.

As the magma slowly cools, it forms igneous rock, such as granite.

Sandstone changes to quartzite.

Limestone changes to marble

Mudstone changes to slate.

A batholith is a large mass of magma that pushes its way into upper layers of rock.

▲ CHANGING ROCK

A large mass of slowly cooling liquid rock pushes up through layers of sedimentary rock beneath Earth's surface. This movement creates enough heat and pressure to melt the nearby layers. The metamorphic rocks that form have different colors, mineral grain sizes, and hardness than the sedimentary rocks they used to be.

THE WORLD'S MOST PERFECT MARBLE?

Marble comes in many colors: green, red, pink, blue, and even black. Thick veins of contrasting minerals can give it different textures. The different colors and textures come from mineral impurities that arise when the marble forms. A lack of impurities results in uniform white marble. The large block of marble that Michelangelo eventually carved into *David* came from the marble quarry of Carrara, located in what is now northwestern Italy. This quarry was famous during the Renaissance and still is today for its pure, dazzlingly white marble.

Sawing off flat blocks rather than uneven chunks makes the marble easier to transport, stack, and use in a wide variety of applications.

A worker checks the marble to ensure it has no faults or staining minerals.

MICHELANGELO'S *DAVID* ▼

Michelangelo was an Italian Renaissance artist most famous for his religious paintings on the ceiling of the Sistine Chapel in Vatican City and for this marble sculpture, *David*, located in Florence. Michelangelo carved *David* from a single block of Carrara marble. He completed the sculpture in 1504, at the age of 29. However, he was not the first artist to tackle the job. Other Florentine artists had already tried sculpting the same block of brilliant white marble decades before.

did you know?
AT 17 FEET (5.17 M), ABOUT 6 TONS, AND MORE THAN 500 YEARS OF AGE, *DAVID'S* ANKLES SHOW SIGNS OF STRESS.

Michelangelo imagined that when he carved a piece of marble, he was "freeing" the sculpture "imprisoned" in the stone.

MARS

Mars has always captured people's imaginations. In the nineteenth century, an Italian astronomer described what he called "canalis" on the surface of Mars. Later, an American scientist translated the term as "canals," implying that they had been made by "intelligent beings." Although some people still believe Martians exist, none of the missions to Mars has returned any evidence to support this theory. In truth, Mars is a small planet whose surface has been shaped by volcanoes, quakes, dust storms, and impacts from meteors. It is very cold, on average between −135°F and 26°F (about −93°C and −3°C). Its atmosphere is about 95 percent carbon dioxide, making it unsuitable for human life. Mars exploration began in the 1960s and continues to this day using unpiloted machines called *space probes*. In 2008, NASA's Mars lander, Phoenix, reached the surface of the planet and transmitted information about its climate and geology to Earth for 5 months. Phoenix confirmed the presence of water ice on Mars, and not just a little ice. There is enough frozen water to fill Lake Michigan twice!

did you know? THE LENGTH OF ONE MARTIAN YEAR IS APPROXIMATELY EQUAL TO 687 EARTH DAYS.

GIANT DUST STORMS ▶

Huge dust storms have been known to envelop Mars in a matter of weeks. For example, in 2001, Hubble Space Telescope images showed the beginning of one such dust storm. For more than 3 months, scientists observed as the dust storm grew until it blanketed the whole planet. During this time, the air temperature on Mars rose 54°F (30°C).

Mars is often called the Red Planet because its soil has iron oxide in it.

Solar System

Mercury   Earth   Jupiter   Saturn   Uranus   Neptune

Venus   Mars

Sun

Mars is the fourth planet from the Sun. This image shows the order of the planets and their approximate sizes relative to one another.

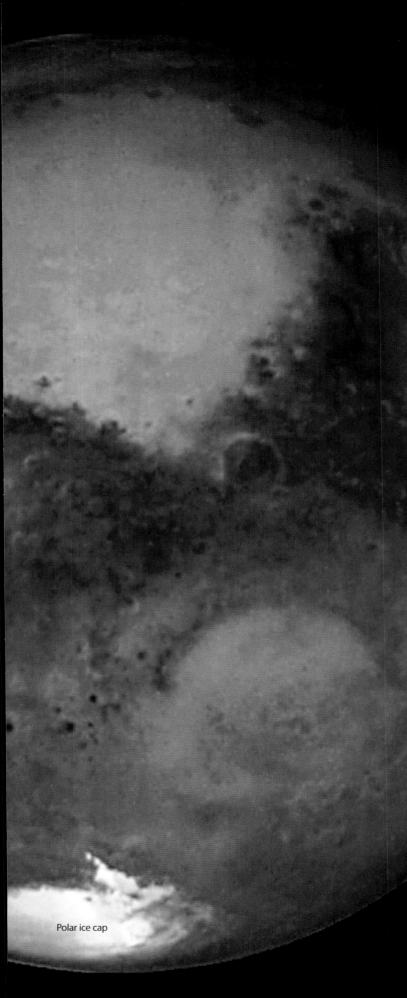

Polar ice cap

Olympus Mons is about as wide as the state of New Mexico, and is about 15 miles (25 km) tall. That's almost three times as tall as Mt. Everest!

▲ THE BIGGEST VOLCANO

Mars is about half the size of Earth, but it has perhaps the largest volcano in our solar system—Olympus Mons. Most volcanoes on Mars are 10 to 100 times larger than those on Earth.

Gullies possibly made by flowing water

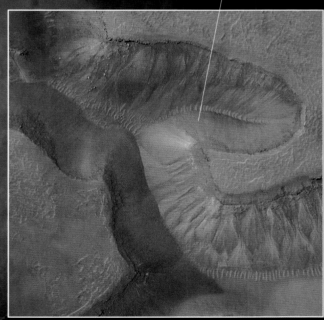

▲ IS THERE LIQUID WATER ON MARS?

The Martian temperature is too cold for liquid water to exist on the surface. However, scientists think that liquid water may have flowed on the surface of Mars hundreds of billions of years ago when the planet was warmer than it is today.

MARS ROVER

Can you imagine traveling to Mars? That would be a long trip! But before people can land on Mars, unpiloted machines have to explore the planet. Spirit and Opportunity are two robots, called *rovers*, sent to Mars by NASA in 2003 to collect information on the planet. They are still there, exploring dry riverbeds, rocks that form only when water is present, and even what some scientists think was an ocean that existed millions of years ago. The measurements the rovers make, using a variety of instruments and computers, can help scientists learn how water helped shape the Martian landscape.

Navigation cameras, with which engineers can control movement from Earth

Panoramic cameras allow the rover to see in the distance and 360 degrees in all directions.

Mast for cameras

Hazard avoidance camera, used in automated navigation

A ROVER'S ARM ▲

The arm of the rover can perform many tasks. It has several instruments for measuring and analyzing soil and rock samples. It can take microscopic images of rocks, study magnetic minerals in dust particles, analyze the chemistry of rocks, and grind the surface to expose the rock's interior to the instruments. The arm even has a small brush to clean the drill bit before it grinds the next sample!

Mechanical arm

Instruments on arm

SPIRIT'S ROUTE ▶

You can see Spirit's route from its landing site to Bonneville Crater. While working, Spirit broke its right front wheel. This turned out to be a lucky event. By dragging the broken wheel, Spirit opened a trench, exposing the ground under the surface. Scientists could then study the composition of the subsurface soil. They concluded that minerals such as sulfur and silica could only have been deposited there by hot water.

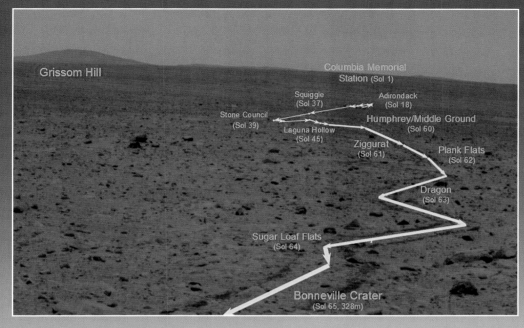

Grissom Hill

Columbia Memorial Station (Sol 1)

Squiggle (Sol 37)

Adirondack (Sol 18)

Stone Council (Sol 39)

Humphrey/Middle Ground (Sol 60)

Laguna Hollow (Sol 45)

Ziggurat (Sol 61)

Plank Flats (Sol 62)

Dragon (Sol 63)

Sugar Loaf Flats (Sol 64)

Bonneville Crater (Sol 65, 328m)

The low-gain antenna can transmit information to spacecraft orbiting Mars, which then relay the information to Earth.

The steerable high-gain antenna can direct information to antennas on Earth.

did you
know? ....
THE MARS ROVERS WERE DESIGNED FOR A 3-MONTH MISSION, BUT THEY ARE STILL COLLECTING AND SENDING INFORMATION TO EARTH AFTER 5 YEARS!

Solar panels

A rocker mobility system keeps rovers from tipping over.

Ridged wheels

◀ ROVER ANATOMY

Each Mars rover has 9 cameras—6 for navigation and 3 for scientific investigation. Two antennas transmit information to and from Earth. Solar panels, charged by sunlight, provide the rover's main source of energy. Ridged wheels allow these robots to move over Mars's sandy and rocky surface. The powerful hardware and software on board can assess when to stop to avoid a hazard or to investigate something of interest. The on-board computer has been programmed by NASA to do such things as open landing gear, periodically take the rover's temperature, test its communication systems, process data from its cameras, and reboot itself. Controllers on the ground can update the software and send specific instructions in response to data they receive from the rover. Spirit's wheels recently became stuck in soft ground, but its instrumentation continued to gather data.

MARSUPIALS

You may use your pocket for carrying a phone or a wallet. A marsupial mother uses her pocket to care for her newborn. Marsupials, which include kangaroos, possums, koalas, wallabies, wombats, sugar gliders, opossums, and Tasmanian devils, are mammals that carry their young in a pouch on their bodies. Marsupials are much less developed than other mammals when they are born. They are too weak to survive outside of the mother's body. Instead, they crawl into the mother's pouch. There, they drink milk, stay warm, and grow strong enough to finally leave after several weeks or months. All living things have adaptations—special body parts or behaviors that help them survive. Newborn marsupials have very strong, well-developed front limbs and paws. This important adaptation lets them grasp tightly onto their mother's fur and make the tough climb to her pouch.

◄ RING-TAILED POSSUM

The ring-tailed possum of Australia is a nocturnal marsupial, active at night and asleep during the day. At home in the trees, ring-tailed possums have strong tails that can coil around branches and act as a fifth limb. Possums in Australia are different from opossums, which are found only in North and South America. In the United States, people often use the name *possum* as a shortened form of the word *opossum*. But opossums are different animals in a different order from the Australian animal called a possum. The saying "playing possum" comes from the Virginia opossum. When a dangerous enemy is near, they lie on their back and stick out their tongue, pretending to be dead.

did you know?
WHILE THE ADULT OPOSSUM IS AS LARGE AS A HOUSE CAT, ITS NEWBORNS ARE THE SIZE OF THE TIP OF YOUR PINKY FINGER.

◄ WALLABY

Wallabies are similar to kangaroos, only smaller. Most grow to be only 1 or 2 feet tall (about 30–61 cm). Like kangaroos, wallabies are found in Australia. They jump using their strong hind legs and big feet. Wallabies' long, thick tails help them keep their balance. A young wallaby, called a *joey*, spends a few months in its mother's pouch, drinking her nourishing milk. When it grows up, a wallaby eats grasses and other plants found in the bushy forests where they live.

The large hind legs of wallabies and kangaroos allow them to move by saltation—hopping with their back feet.

When joeys are old enough to survive outside of their mother's pouch, they sometimes return to hide from danger.

A koala's nose is dark and leathery.

Koalas have fuzzy, grey-white fur that feels like a sheep's wool.

KOALA ►

Like most of the world's marsupials, koalas are found in Australia. They spend most of their time in eucalyptus trees, eating and napping. While the leaves of the eucalyptus are poisonous to most other animals, it is the only food that koalas will eat. They eat from 1 to 3 pounds (about 0.5 to 1.4 kg) of leaves per day. They even smell like their food—kind of like cough drops. A young koala lives in its mother's pouch for 6 months, drinking her milk. Then it spends another 6 months clinging to her fur while learning to eat leaves.

MEASUREMENT

How fast can an airplane fly? How far is it to your friend's house? How tall are you? All these questions can be answered through measurement. Speed, distance, and height are measurements. So are weight, volume, and temperature. To describe a measurement, you must use a number value and the correct units. Two common systems of units are metric, or International System of Units (SI), and customary. Miles, inches, pounds, gallons, and ounces are customary units. Kilometers, centimeters, grams, and liters are metric units. The metric system, based on the number 10, was devised in the 1790s to bring order to conflicting measurement systems used in Europe. The United States is one of only a few countries to retain the customary system, which is derived from the English and Imperial systems. However, all countries use the metric system as the common language of international trade, commerce, and science.

did you know?..............................
IN 1999, A NASA MARS ORBITER WAS LOST BECAUSE DIFFERENT TEAMS ACCIDENTALLY USED DIFFERENT UNITS OF MEASUREMENT DURING A MISSION.

A London double-decker bus is about 28 feet (8.5 m) long and weighs about 16,600 pounds (about 7,530 kg).

UNITS OF MEASUREMENT ▶

Scientists use measurements to compare objects. But in order to compare two objects, the units of their measurements must be from the same system. Often, scientists have to convert measurements from customary units to metric units and vice versa. For example, the metric unit of weight is the kilogram (kg), while the customary unit is the pound (lb), 1 kg = 2.2046 lb. The metric unit of length is the meter (m), while the customary unit is the foot (ft), 1 m = 3.28084 ft.

Adult male sperm whales can grow to about 60 feet (18 m) long and weigh about 90,000 pounds (40,800 kg).

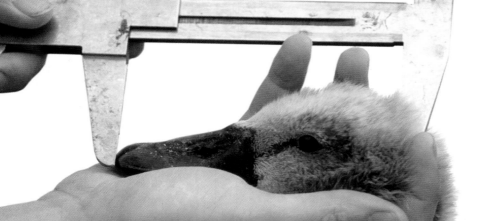

◀ INSTRUMENTS FOR MEASURING

People need to measure things all the time. They want to know if an object will fit in a box, if something is too heavy to carry in a backpack, or how much an animal has grown. Chemists measure the amount of solution, physicists measure the brightness of a light bulb, and carpenters measure the length of a board. All these measurements are made with instruments designed for a specific purpose. Calipers, shown to the left, are used to measure the length or thickness of small objects. You slide the measuring points together or apart until they just touch each end of the object being measured. Then you can read the units between the measuring points.

REFLECTING BACK ▶

A laser reflector left on the moon by Apollo 11 astronauts in 1969 enables scientists to take very precise measurements in space by bouncing laser beams off the device. Scientists have learned, for example, that the moon—on average about 239,228 miles (385,000 km) from Earth—is slowly moving away from Earth at a rate of about 1.5 inches (3.8 cm) per year

The reflector is a square about 18 inches (46 cm) on a side.

LASER RANGING TELESCOPE ▼

A satellite laser ranging (SLR) telescope in England shines a laser beam at a satellite. A reflector on the satellite reflects the beam back to Earth. By measuring the time it takes the beam to return, scientists can track the distance to the satellite. Tracking this distance over time lets scientists detect slight changes in Earth's rotation.

The laser beam shines through the telescope and is expanded by the lens or mirror in the telescope.

MELTING POINT

Knowing the melting point of a solid—the temperature at which it becomes a liquid—helps you make decisions all the time. You put bread in a toaster, but you don't insert a bar of chocolate. You bake cookies on a sheet made of metal, not plastic. Generally, you expect solids to stay solid. You take for granted that your lunch will not melt in your backpack and your bicycle will not melt in the sun. Scientists use the melting point of a substance as a way to identify an unknown chemical or to determine which material to use for a particular task. A scientist can determine each ingredient in a tablet or pill by measuring the temperature at which each substance melts. To make clothing, utensils, electronic devices, and most everything we use each day, manufacturers choose the material based partly on its melting point.

Chocolate starts out as a thick liquid made of roasted, ground cocoa beans. It is molded into solid shapes as it cools.

MELTS IN YOUR MOUTH ►

Chocolate is made up of about half fat, called *cocoa butter*, and half cocoa particles—similar to dry cocoa powder. When you melt chocolate, the cocoa butter melts. The change is physical, because the cocoa butter will harden again at room temperature. The melting point of chocolate is just below your body temperature of around 98.6°F (37°C). When the chocolate melts on your tongue, it absorbs thermal energy from your mouth, which is an endothermic change.

The flame keeps burning as long as it has fuel and oxygen.

The wax drip on the candle's side has gone through two physical changes: melting and solidifying.

know?
did you

....
TUNGSTEN METAL HAS THE HIGHEST MELTING POINT OF THE METALLIC ELEMENTS: 6,152°F (3,410°C). IT IS USED TO MAKE THE THIN WIRE THAT GLOWS IN LIGHT BULBS.

◄ KEEPING A FLAME BURNING

The flame of a candle produces plenty of heat to cause wax to melt. Candle wax melts at a temperature of about 150°F (about 66°C) and the flame is around 2,552°F (1,400°C). The liquid wax travels up the candle's wick. The flame heats the molecules of liquid wax so that they vibrate fast enough to vaporize into a gas. After these two physical changes—melting and vaporizing—a chemical change takes place. The chemical bonds between the atoms of the gaseous wax break. The atoms bond with the oxygen in the air, and combustion, or burning, takes place. This exothermic reaction releases energy in the form of heat and light.

Most iron is found in iron ore, which consists of rocks and minerals surrounding the iron.

The material used to hold the molten iron has to have a melting point higher than that of iron.

The melting point of iron is 2,800°F (about 1,538°C).

MOLTEN IRON ▶

Iron and other metals can be melted, poured into molds, and cooled. These are physical changes. Other molten metals can be added to molten iron to produce solid solutions called *alloys*. The atoms of the two metals remain unchanged, so making an alloy is a physical change. Combining small amounts of carbon and other elements with iron makes various types of steel, which is an alloy. This combining can add certain desirable qualities to the alloy, such as strength or flexibility.

Molten iron is poured into a mold to solidify. The solid piece of iron is called an *ingot*.

MENSTRUAL CYCLE

One sign that a girl's body is in the process of sexual development is a pattern of changes that repeats about once a month, called the *menstrual cycle.* Her endocrine system begins to secrete hormones to control these changes. First her hypothalamus sends a signal to her pituitary gland. Just as the hypothalamus sends messages about other bodily activities, such as hunger or the need for sleep, it signals her pituitary gland to begin the reproductive process. The pituitary gland then secretes hormones that cause several of the egg-containing structures in the ovaries, called *follicles*, to grow larger. As they mature, the follicles release the hormone called *estrogen.* When estrogen levels are high enough, the pituitary gland again releases hormones that cause a mature follicle to release its egg. This process is called *ovulation*, and it takes place in the middle of the menstrual cycle.

MENSTRUATION ►

Estrogen causes the lining of the uterus to become thicker, with extra tissue and blood, so it is ready to nourish a fertilized egg. Once the follicle has released the egg, it closes and forms a structure called the *corpus luteum.* This structure produces more hormones that build up the lining of the uterus. If fertilization does not occur, the uterus sheds its extra tissue and blood through the vagina—called *menstruation*, or a *period*—and the cycle begins again.

did you know?
ALTHOUGH IT CAN SEEM LIKE MORE, THE AVERAGE AMOUNT OF BLOOD LOST PER PERIOD IS ABOUT 2 TO 3 TABLESPOONS (30 TO 40 ML).

SUNDAY MONDAY TUESDAY WEDNESDAY THURSDAY FRIDAY SATURDAY

An unfertilized egg results in menstrual bleeding, the first day of a new menstrual cycle.

The new cycle's egg inside follicle

Follicle growing

Ovulation (follicle releasing egg)

Mature follicle

Corpus luteum, formed from the empty follicle, secreting hormones

Corpus luteum shrinking if egg is not fertilized

Cycle repeating, with menstrual bleeding after egg is not fertilized

The average menstrual cycle is 28 days, but it can be 21 to 45 days.

1 2 3 4 5 6 7 8 9 10 11 12 13 14 15 16 17 18 19 20 21 22 23 24 25 26 28 29 30

JOURNEY OF AN EGG ▼

A woman usually has two ovaries, one on either side of the uterus. Each is about the size of a grape. During ovulation, an egg is released from a follicle within one of the ovaries. The egg enters a fallopian tube and travels to the uterus. If it is fertilized, it is called a *zygote*, and it can then attach to the uterine wall where the lining has thickened.

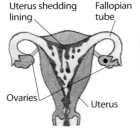

Uterus shedding lining   Fallopian tube

Ovaries   Uterus

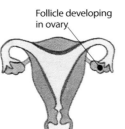

Follicle developing in ovary

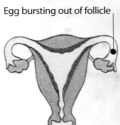

Egg bursting out of follicle

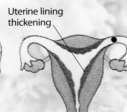

Uterine lining thickening

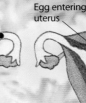

Egg entering uterus

ALL THE EGGS

Every girl begins life with all of her eggs. At birth, there are 1 to 2 million eggs. By puberty, there are about 400,000. Fewer than 500 of these will be released during the woman's lifetime, and the rest will disintegrate as she ages. As hormone levels begin to decline, usually between ages 45 and 55, the woman's menstrual cycle stops.

If you could stand on the planet Mercury and look up at the sky, the sun would appear almost three times larger than it does on Earth. However, you would need a specially made spacesuit to protect you. Mercury is so close to the sun that it receives much more heat, light, and dangerous radiation than other planets in our solar system. Its surface temperatures are as high as 806°F (almost 430°C) when the sun is shining and as low as –274°F (almost –170°C) at night. These extraordinary temperatures occur because Mercury has almost no atmosphere. There are not enough gases to trap the sun's heat near the planet's surface at night or to shield it during the day, the way Earth's atmosphere does. Current evidence even suggests that Mercury, the planet closest to the sun, has icy poles. The deep craters at the poles are in permanent shade. Thus, water at the bottom of these craters is always frozen.

did you know?

MERCURY ZIPS AROUND THE SUN IN 88 EARTH DAYS, BUT IT ROTATES SO SLOWLY THAT ONE MERCURY DAY IS TWO THIRDS OF ITS YEAR!

Mercury   Earth   Jupiter   Saturn   Uranus   Neptune

Venus   Mars

Sun

This chart shows the order of the planets. Mercury is closest to the sun.

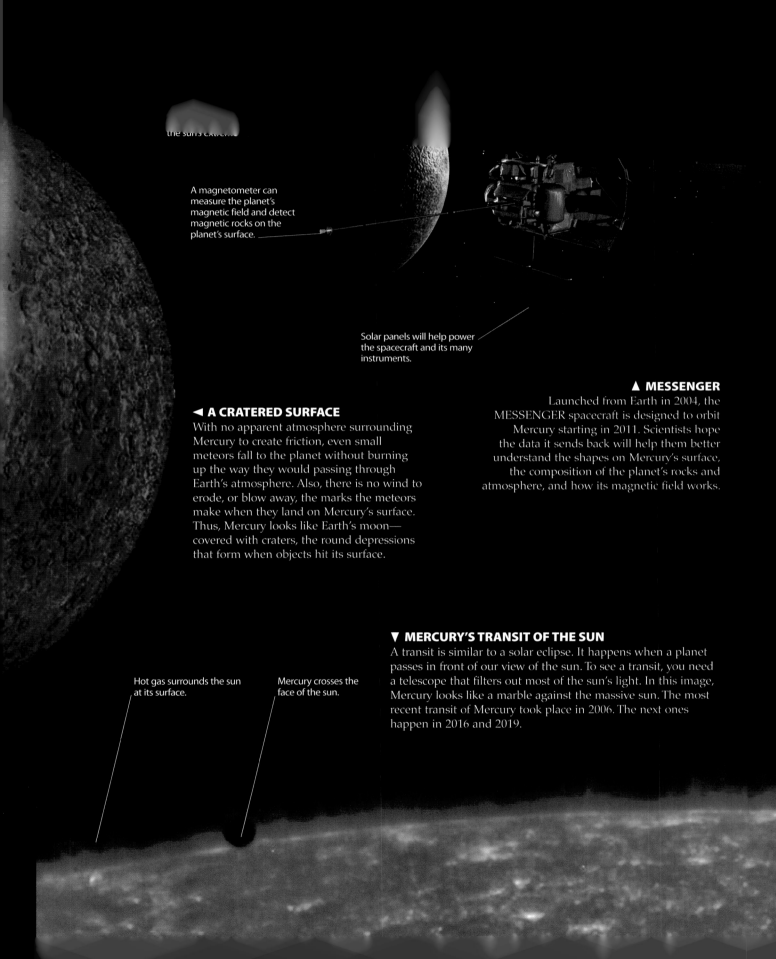

the sun's extreme

A magnetometer can measure the planet's magnetic field and detect magnetic rocks on the planet's surface.

Solar panels will help power the spacecraft and its many instruments.

▲ MESSENGER

Launched from Earth in 2004, the MESSENGER spacecraft is designed to orbit Mercury starting in 2011. Scientists hope the data it sends back will help them better understand the shapes on Mercury's surface, the composition of the planet's rocks and atmosphere, and how its magnetic field works.

◄ A CRATERED SURFACE

With no apparent atmosphere surrounding Mercury to create friction, even small meteors fall to the planet without burning up the way they would passing through Earth's atmosphere. Also, there is no wind to erode, or blow away, the marks the meteors make when they land on Mercury's surface. Thus, Mercury looks like Earth's moon—covered with craters, the round depressions that form when objects hit its surface.

▼ MERCURY'S TRANSIT OF THE SUN

A transit is similar to a solar eclipse. It happens when a planet passes in front of our view of the sun. To see a transit, you need a telescope that filters out most of the sun's light. In this image, Mercury looks like a marble against the massive sun. The most recent transit of Mercury took place in 2006. The next ones happen in 2016 and 2019.

Hot gas surrounds the sun at its surface.

Mercury crosses the face of the sun.

METEORITES

On a clear night, a bright streak shoots across the sky. A chunk of metal or rock has just sped into Earth's atmosphere from space. The chunk slammed into the air, generating so much heat from friction that it began to burn, leaving behind a trail of glowing gas called a *meteor* or a *shooting star.* The upper atmosphere shatters most meteors into tiny bits, but some large rocks may survive and crash into Earth's surface. The pieces that survive are called *meteorites.* In all of human history, a meteorite has struck a person only once. In Alabama in 1954, Ann Hodges was on her couch when an 8.5-pound (3.8-kg) meteorite broke through her roof. A bit bigger—and heavier— than a brick, it hit her hand and hip, creating large bruises.

did you know?
THE LARGEST METEORITE EVER FOUND IS ABOUT 3 FEET (1 m) HIGH AND 8 FEET (2.5 m) WIDE. IT WEIGHS MORE THAN 60 TONS.

Why is an iron meteorite red? The iron reacted with oxygen after it reached Earth. The red color is from rust.

The crater is 570 feet (170 m) deep.

▲ **IRON-NICKEL METEORITE FROM NAMIBIA**
This meteorite was once part of the dense center of a large asteroid. Now it is a small, heavy chunk of iron with a tiny amount of nickel. Meteorites can provide direct evidence of what our solar system was like when it began about 4.6 billion years ago.

METEOR ▶

Meteors fly into the atmosphere at speeds as high as 100,000 miles per hour (160,000 km/h). During a meteor shower, it is sometimes possible to watch 100 meteors bombard our planet each hour. Meteor showers occur when Earth travels through particles left behind by a comet.

The crater rim rises 150 feet (45 m) above the surrounding plains.

▼ IMPACT CRATER IN ARIZONA, USA

The largest impacts from meteorites gouge craters out of our planet. About 50,000 years ago, an iron-nickel meteorite 150 feet (45 m) across smashed into northern Arizona. Within seconds, the impact melted and pushed out all the nearby rock with enough explosive force to dig out this crater, 4,000 feet (1,200 m) in diameter. The meteorite itself shattered into tiny bits of metal. These dense fragments sank into the lighter molten rock. Soon the rock above cooled and turned into a solid again. Today, geologists believe small pieces of the original meteorite are trapped deep below the crater floor.

Crystals of the mineral olivine are embedded in iron.

▲ STONY-IRON METEORITE FROM ARGENTINA

The mixture of stone and metal in this meteorite provides geologists with good evidence about its origins. It was once part of the region where an asteroid's core and crust met. The stony parts, including the olivine, came from the asteroid's lighter crust, and the iron parts are from the asteroid's dense core.

MICROSCOPES

Most people can see something as small as a human hair. But if you want to examine the tiny hairs on an ant, you need a microscope. A microscope is a tool used to see things that are too small to see with your eyes alone. The microscopes in most science classrooms are light microscopes. They focus light using curved pieces of glass, or lenses. Light microscopes are useful for viewing objects only as small as a cell. To see something smaller, like an atom, you need an electron microscope. An electron microscope uses a beam of electrons to magnify a sample. Transmission electron microscopes (TEMs) detect how electrons interact with the sample as they travel through it. They produce two-dimensional views that look like cross sections. Scanning electron microscopes (SEMs) detect electrons that bounce off the sample's surface, which has been covered with a thin layer of metal, usually gold. They produce three-dimensional images.

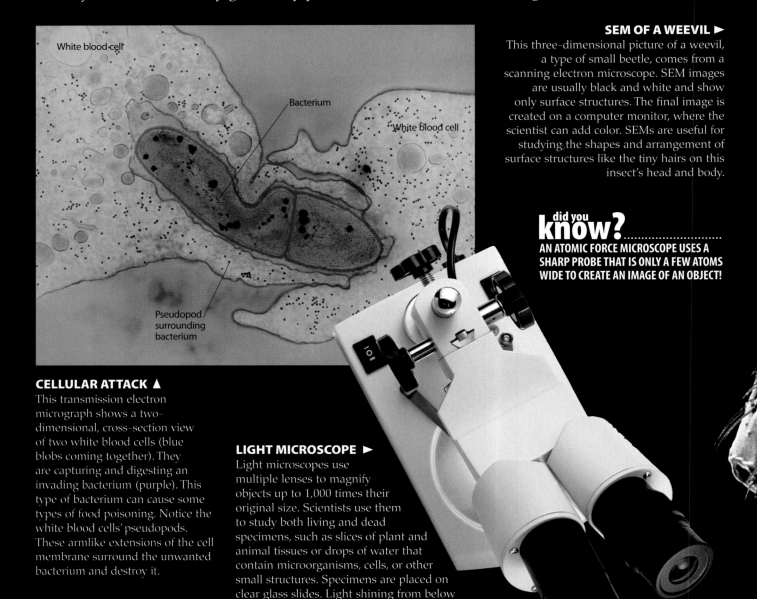

White blood cell

Bacterium

White blood cell

Pseudopod surrounding bacterium

SEM OF A WEEVIL ▶

This three-dimensional picture of a weevil, a type of small beetle, comes from a scanning electron microscope. SEM images are usually black and white and show only surface structures. The final image is created on a computer monitor, where the scientist can add color. SEMs are useful for studying the shapes and arrangement of surface structures like the tiny hairs on this insect's head and body.

did you know?..........................
AN ATOMIC FORCE MICROSCOPE USES A SHARP PROBE THAT IS ONLY A FEW ATOMS WIDE TO CREATE AN IMAGE OF AN OBJECT!

CELLULAR ATTACK ▲

This transmission electron micrograph shows a two-dimensional, cross-section view of two white blood cells (blue blobs coming together). They are capturing and digesting an invading bacterium (purple). This type of bacterium can cause some types of food poisoning. Notice the white blood cells' pseudopods. These armlike extensions of the cell membrane surround the unwanted bacterium and destroy it.

LIGHT MICROSCOPE ▶

Light microscopes use multiple lenses to magnify objects up to 1,000 times their original size. Scientists use them to study both living and dead specimens, such as slices of plant and animal tissues or drops of water that contain microorganisms, cells, or other small structures. Specimens are placed on clear glass slides. Light shining from below or above illuminates them.

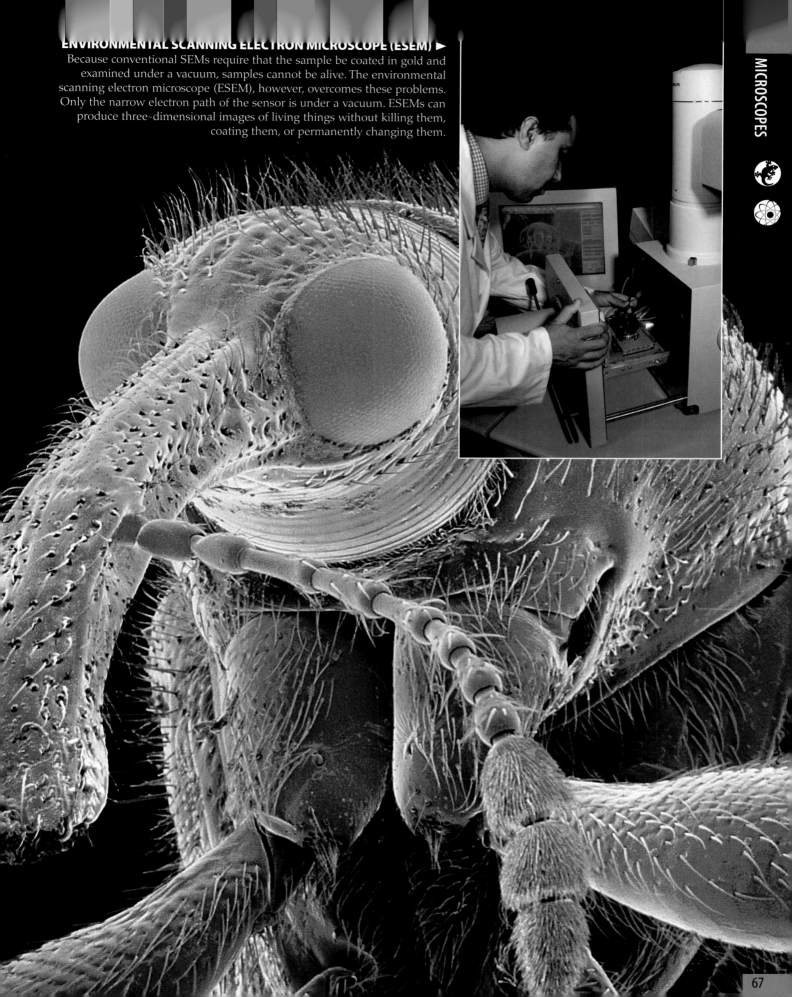

ENVIRONMENTAL SCANNING ELECTRON MICROSCOPE (ESEM) ▶

Because conventional SEMs require that the sample be coated in gold and examined under a vacuum, samples cannot be alive. The environmental scanning electron microscope (ESEM), however, overcomes these problems. Only the narrow electron path of the sensor is under a vacuum. ESEMs can produce three-dimensional images of living things without killing them, coating them, or permanently changing them.

MID-OCEAN RIDGE

Some of the most dynamic parts of Earth's surface are also some of the least known. Mid-ocean ridges occur where Earth's tectonic plates are stretched and pulled apart. Oceanic plates move away from one another at amazingly slow rates of about 0.4 to 8 inches (1 to 20 cm) per year. The movement makes an opening down to the hot magma below. As the plates separate, this magma, or molten rock, bubbles up through the opening, creating mountain ranges. Almost all of these mountains are completely under water. They form a ridge system that winds around the planet in a chain that is more than 40,000 miles (about 65,000 km) long. On average, the top of the ridge is more than 1¼ miles (2,000 m) beneath the ocean's surface, deeper than the Grand Canyon. In some places, such as Iceland, the ridge extends above sea level, and appears as islands with volcanoes.

did you know?......................
THE STRING OF MID-OCEAN RIDGES RUNNING THROUGH THE WORLD'S OCEANS MAKE UP THE LONGEST MOUNTAIN CHAIN ON EARTH.

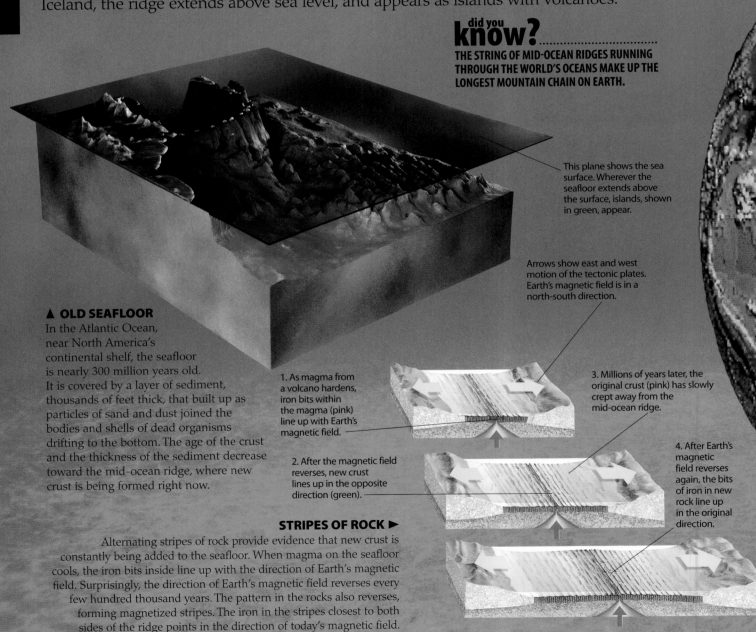

This plane shows the sea surface. Wherever the seafloor extends above the surface, islands, shown in green, appear.

Arrows show east and west motion of the tectonic plates. Earth's magnetic field is in a north-south direction.

▲ OLD SEAFLOOR

In the Atlantic Ocean, near North America's continental shelf, the seafloor is nearly 300 million years old. It is covered by a layer of sediment, thousands of feet thick, that built up as particles of sand and dust joined the bodies and shells of dead organisms drifting to the bottom. The age of the crust and the thickness of the sediment decrease toward the mid-ocean ridge, where new crust is being formed right now.

1. As magma from a volcano hardens, iron bits within the magma (pink) line up with Earth's magnetic field.

2. After the magnetic field reverses, new crust lines up in the opposite direction (green).

3. Millions of years later, the original crust (pink) has slowly crept away from the mid-ocean ridge.

4. After Earth's magnetic field reverses again, the bits of iron in new rock line up in the original direction.

STRIPES OF ROCK ▶

Alternating stripes of rock provide evidence that new crust is constantly being added to the seafloor. When magma on the seafloor cools, the iron bits inside line up with the direction of Earth's magnetic field. Surprisingly, the direction of Earth's magnetic field reverses every few hundred thousand years. The pattern in the rocks also reverses, forming magnetized stripes. The iron in the stripes closest to both sides of the ridge points in the direction of today's magnetic field. Stripes of older rock have been pushed farther from the ridge.

NEW SEAFLOOR

The Mid-Atlantic Ridge extends from the Arctic, through Iceland, and south nearly to Antarctica, dividing the Atlantic Ocean. Along this ridge, seafloor spreading occurs—new crust forms as magma oozes through weak places in the crust. As this crust moves east and west, it cools and slowly sinks so that the ocean on either side of the ridge is much deeper. You might think that the Mid-Atlantic Ridge is a place with no life. This is not the case, however. Hydrothermal vents provide hot water, rich in minerals from magma. An entire ecosystem lives near these places in the ridge where the minerals in the heated water provide energy for living things.

The depth of the ocean is shown by color—darker blue is deeper water. The Mid-Atlantic Ridge shows up as a light blue line splitting the seafloor.

Continental shelf

Iceland

Antarctica

MILKY WAY

The Milky Way is a galaxy—a vast group of stars, dust, gas, planets, and asteroids pulled together by the force of gravity. It contains more than 100 billion stars and planets, including the sun and the rest of our solar system. The Milky Way is more than 100,000 light-years long! A light-year is the distance light travels in one year (5.88 trillion miles, or 9.46 trillion km), so the Milky Way is enormous! The Milky Way formed more than 13 billion years ago. To the naked eye, it looks like a broad white band in the night sky. Ancient people thought this white band looked like a river of milk, so they named it the Milky Way.

did you know? OUR SUN IS LOCATED ABOUT 26,000 LIGHT-YEARS AWAY FROM THE CENTER OF THE MILKY WAY!

SPIRAL GALAXY ▶

The Milky Way is a spiral galaxy, a galaxy shaped like a pinwheel. A spiral galaxy's arms coil outward from the center and are regions where stars form. Thousands of hot, young, blue and blue-white stars give the arms a bright appearance. Like all spiral galaxies, the Milky Way slowly rotates—so slowly it takes about 250 million years for our sun to circle the galaxy's center!

Young blue and blue-white stars shine much brighter than older, redder stars.

BARRED SPIRAL GALAXY ▲

Scientists believe there are more than 100 billion galaxies in the universe. The common barred spiral galaxy has a band of bright stars that emerges from the center and extends across the middle of the galaxy. About half of all spiral galaxies are barred. Many scientists believe the Milky Way is a barred spiral galaxy.

THE SOMBRERO GALAXY ▲

From Earth, we can see the Sombrero galaxy only edge-on. Its flat disk and bulging center, formed by billions of old glowing stars, give the galaxy its hatlike appearance. Bands of dust form the disk's dark rings. Scientists do not fully understand them, but believe the rings contain younger and brighter stars. They also believe the center of the galaxy holds a large black hole.

THE MILKY ROAD ▼

This image was created from different photos, to make the Milky Way look as though it extended out from the end of a road. From Earth, the Milky Way does not look this colorful. Also, it is difficult to see, especially in cities where the night sky is filled with light from cars, buildings, and streetlights.

At the center of the Milky Way may be a black hole a million times larger than the sun.

MIRAGES

In just about any cartoon that takes place in the desert, a hot, thirsty character sees an inviting pool of water in the middle of a burning expanse of sand. But what the character actually sees is a mirage, not a pool of water. A mirage is an image of a distant object that is caused by refraction—light waves changing speed as they pass from one medium into another, causing the light to bend. The mirage is real in the sense that it is an optical phenomenon, like a rainbow, that can be photographed by a camera. When you look out at an expanse of hot sand or highway, you might see a shiny, bluish surface on the ground. You are actually seeing an image of the sky, which looks as if there were a mirror lying on the ground. But the sky on the ground makes no sense, so your brain interprets the image as something that might actually form on the ground—a pool of water.

A LAKE IN THE DESERT?

Mirages are especially convincing in places like the Namib Desert in Africa. Mirages occur where the eye can see across a relatively flat surface for some distance. Here, the trees appear to be reflected in a lake. What looks like a lake is the result of light bending as it passes through layers of air that are at different temperatures. For a mirage to occur, the light has to be hitting the hot desert surface and the trees at a certain angle, typically from lower in the sky. The light that bounces off distant objects is refracted as it passes from the cooler air at eye level to the hotter air on the desert floor.

The mirage of the trees and sand is seen below the trees and sand, so it is called an *inferior mirage.*

Light refracted as it passes through the hot air above the desert appears as a lake.

WET ROAD AHEAD ▶

Where did that puddle come from on a hot, dry day? Black pavement doesn't reflect images, so it has to be water that you see, reflecting the motorcycles and car up ahead. As you draw closer, however, the water disappears. That's because there never was any water—you saw a mirage!

1. Light rays usually travel in a straight line.

2. This ray coming from the top of the tree begins bending when it hits the hot air.

3. The light ray is bent upward by hot air.

4. The bent light ray enters the eye in a straight line, so it appears to have originated from a point on the ground, as if it had traveled in a straight (dashed) line.

Real object

Layer of cool air

Layer of hot air

Mirage

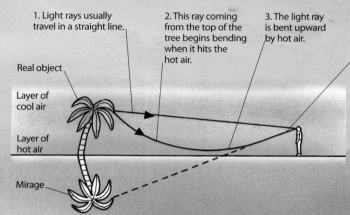

did you know?
....
MIRAGES CAN OCCUR ABOVE COLD SURFACES, SUCH AS THE OCEAN, ICE, OR SNOW. ON THE OCEAN, ISLANDS CAN APPEAR TO BE FLOATING ABOVE THE HORIZON. WHEN A MIRAGE IS SEEN ABOVE THE ACTUAL OBJECT, IT IS CALLED A *SUPERIOR MIRAGE*.

HOW IT WORKS ▲

Light rays bounce off a tree in the distance. The rays travel through layers of air. Usually the light rays travel in a straight line. The layer of air right next to the sand is much hotter than the layer of air above it. Light travels faster through hot air, which is less dense than cool air. The light rays that pass from cool air to hot air travel faster, so they refract. These rays bend upward toward the viewer's eye, rather than continuing on the path they were on in the cool layer, forming a mirage.

Light travels directly to your eye to form an image of the tree in the distance.

Light refracted through the layer of hot air creates an inverted image.

MOLD

Have you ever opened the refrigerator for a snack only to find nasty green fur, gray splotches, orange fuzz, or white dusty stuff on something you were hoping to eat? This is mold, a type of fungus. Mold doesn't just grow on food; it can also grow on plants, paper, and even walls. Like the vast body of an iceberg sitting below the surface of the water, most of a mold is hidden under the surface on which it grows. The part of the mold that you can see contains microscopic spores that will be released into the air by the millions. Mold spores are all around you—in the air that you breathe, and on virtually every surface. Some molds can cause allergic reactions and respiratory infections. They thrive in damp, warm areas, but spores can survive almost anywhere until the conditions are just right for them to grow!

BATTLE OF THE MOLD! ▼

The thousands of homes and businesses flooded by Hurricanes Katrina and Rita in 2005 provided the perfect conditions for mold to grow. Because buildings stayed wet for so long, mold took over, covering any surfaces it could. Efforts to remove the mold were not always successful.

did you know?..............................
A STUFFY NOSE AND ITCHY EYES MIGHT BE AN ALLERGIC REACTION TO MOLD. MOLDS CAN ALSO CAUSE ASTHMA ATTACKS.

The threadlike "roots" (hyphae) of molds can be hard to see. They can be deep inside contaminated foods, wood, or fabric.

Mold spores in high concentrations can cause health problems. Face masks and gloves were necessary to protect workers during the massive cleanup operation.

Carpets, cupboards, tables, walls, and floors—all were attacked by molds after the flooding.

NOT QUITE SO PEACHY! ▶

It's bad enough when mold invades your fruit bowl, but on a large scale it can be a farmer's worst enemy. Crops can be wiped out by mold if storage conditions are not right or if the weather turns damp too early. However, some molds are useful in food production. Blue-veined cheeses like Stilton get their coloring and taste from mold. Mold is also used when making soy sauce and tempeh.

Stilton cheese

A mold changes in both color and texture as the spores ripen.

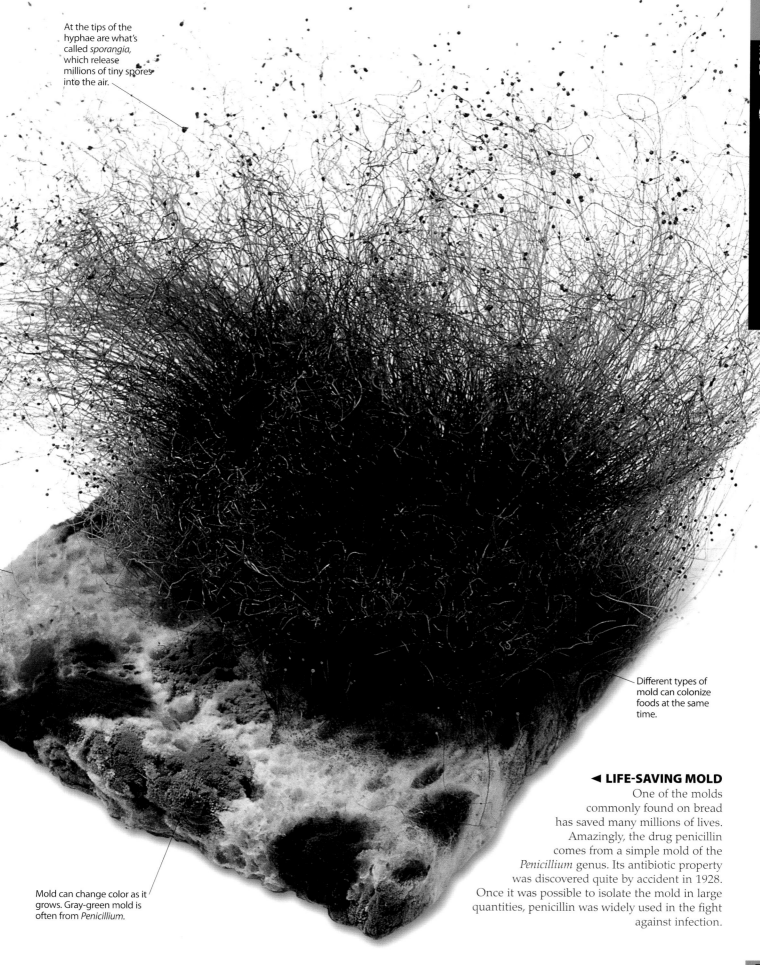

At the tips of the hyphae are what's called *sporangia,* which release millions of tiny spores into the air.

Different types of mold can colonize foods at the same time.

Mold can change color as it grows. Gray-green mold is often from *Penicillium.*

◄ LIFE-SAVING MOLD

One of the molds commonly found on bread has saved many millions of lives. Amazingly, the drug penicillin comes from a simple mold of the *Penicillium* genus. Its antibiotic property was discovered quite by accident in 1928. Once it was possible to isolate the mold in large quantities, penicillin was widely used in the fight against infection.

ust like most of the other planets, Earth has a sidekick—the moon. A moon is a natural satellite, an object that orbits a planet. Earth is nearly 4 times as wide and about 81 times as heavy as its moon. The moon may not be very big, but it has a big effect on Earth. It reflects the sun's light as moonlight during most nights each month. It also affects the Earth's oceans. The moon's gravity, along with that of the sun, causes tides by pulling on Earth's ocean water, causing it to rise up. Throughout history, telescopes and spacecraft have let scientists study the moon from Earth. In the last century, 12 people actually got to visit the moon. Between July of 1969 and December of 1972, American astronauts made 6 successful landings on the moon. On these Apollo missions, astronauts explored the moon's surface, took photographs, collected rock and dust samples, and set up equipment to monitor moon conditions.

◄ **SCARRED SURFACE**

The moon is covered in craters. Craters are the round dents that form when meteors impact, or hit, the moon's dusty surface. The moon has no atmosphere. This means there is no wind or weather to erode these features after they form. The only things that change craters are geologic activity and newer impacts. Scientists can study the craters to figure out the order in which different moon features formed.

The lunar rover, called a "moon buggy" by some, was a small electric car that let astronauts explore the moon.

During a moon landing, the lunar module would carry two astronauts from a spacecraft in orbit around the moon to the moon's surface and back.

In April of 1972, astronaut John Young jumps up as he salutes the American flag during the fifth moon landing.

▲ APOLLO 16 MOON LANDING

The force of gravity is related to how much an object weighs. Because the moon weighs much less than Earth, its gravity is only one sixth that of Earth. Astronauts visiting the moon during the Apollo missions experienced firsthand its reduced gravity. They found it easier to jump and bounce, even while wearing very heavy spacesuits.

▼ MOON OVER EARTH

This photo taken from the International Space Station makes it look as if the moon is in Earth's atmosphere, but it is really only a trick of the light. The moon is actually 238,900 miles (about 384,500 km) away from Earth. During visits to the moon, astronauts have left mirrors there. By bouncing laser light from Earth off these mirrors, scientists can measure exactly how far away the moon is from Earth's surface.

did you know?...

WITH NO WIND, WEATHER, OR LIVING THINGS TO DISTURB THEM, THE EQUIPMENT, DISCARDED VEHICLES, AND EVEN FOOTPRINTS LEFT BY ASTRONAUTS MORE THAN 40 YEARS AGO REMAIN UNCHANGED ON THE MOON'S SURFACE.

Earth's moon

Earth

MOUNT EVEREST

The top of Mount Everest is the highest place on Earth. Its snowcapped peak stands at 29,035 feet (almost 8,850 m) above sea level—and it is still growing! Colliding tectonic plates are pushing the mighty Himalaya Mountains up at a rate of about 5 millimeters per year. Weather conditions at the summit can be extreme, with hurricane-force winds and an average temperature of –33°F (–36°C). Most climbers try for the summit in the spring when conditions are most favorable. But even then, fierce storms can happen suddenly. Even in good weather, glaciers can shift and crack, creating dangerous crevasses. With only one third of the oxygen at sea level available to them, many climbers have died because of these treacherous conditions.

The North Face is one of Everest's three faces, or sides.

Rongbuk glacier

THE YAK ▲

Yaks are huge shaggy beasts well suited to life in the mountains. They have adaptations, such as large lungs and more red blood cells, that allow them to live at high altitudes where oxygen is scarce. Yaks are important to the survival of the people of the Himalayas. They are a source of milk, meat, and fur for warm coats. Their dung is dried and used as fuel, and they are excellent mountain pack animals.

SNOW LEOPARDS ▶

Snow leopards are an endangered species and are very rarely seen in the wild. Between 3,000 and 6,000 of these amazing cats are left in the vastness of the Himalayas. They have been hunted for their beautiful thick fur, and their bones and organs are used in traditional Chinese medicine. Only one snow leopard has been seen on Mount Everest in the past 40 years.

The South Face is the most popular route to the summit.

The border between Nepal and China runs across the top of Everest.

A MOUNTAIN WITH MANY NAMES

In 1865, Mount Everest was named after Sir George Everest, the British Surveyor General of India at the time the mountain was first mapped in 1841. In Nepalese, it is called *Sagarmatha*, "forehead in the sky," and in Tibetan, *Chomolungma*, "goddess mother of the world." The summit was first reached in 1953 after many failed attempts. Now, there are many expeditions up the mountain each year—but not all of them are successful.

▲ A BREATH OF THIN AIR

Climbing Mount Everest is no easy task. Climbers must spend several weeks adapting to the high elevation at Base Camp—around 17,500 feet (5,334 m). They then rest at higher camps over 21,000 feet (6,400 m), acclimating to the lower oxygen levels as they ascend. Most climbers need extra oxygen to reach the summit. Lack of oxygen flow to the brain can make them feel dizzy, sleepy, and confused. At high altitude, this is a serious risk to their lives.

did you know? THE ROCKS THAT FORM THE HIMALAYAS, INCLUDING MOUNT EVEREST, WERE ONCE PART OF THE OCEAN FLOOR!

MP3 PLAYER

Pick a song, any song. MP3 players have revolutionized the music industry by allowing us to download songs of our choice and store many of them together in a small space. An MP3, an abbreviation for a type of file—MPEG audio layer 3—is a digital file that stores songs in a compressed form. The algorithm, or formula, used to compress MP3 files takes out sounds that the human ear cannot hear. For example, when two sounds play at once we hear only the louder one, so MP3 files eliminate the softer sound. This makes files at least ten times smaller. Some listeners prefer to compress the files less in order to preserve more of the sound quality.

FULLY PORTABLE ▼

In the 1980s, when boomboxes like the one shown below were popular, bigger was considered better. These boxes could weigh in at 20 pounds (9 kg). MP3 players that easily fit in your pocket have given new meaning to the word *portable*. Most use rechargeable lithium batteries that can last up to 36 hours on a charge. MP3 players that are about the size of a pack of cards typically weigh about 4–9 ounces (120–250 g), but some tiny ones weigh only 0.38 ounces (10.7 g). The smallest players have 2 gigabytes of memory, which means they can hold 500 or more songs. Standard size players can store about 80 times that number—up to 40,000 songs!

did you know?

THE MORE COMPRESSED AN MP3 FILE IS, THE LESS SPACE IT TAKES UP AND THE FASTER IT IS TO CREATE. THE LESS COMPRESSED IT IS, THE HIGHER THE QUALITY OF THE SOUND.

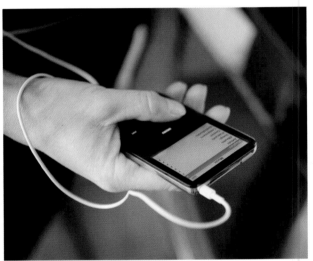

You can browse the Internet using some MP3 players.

Touch a button and watch a movie. Up to 200 hours of video can be stored on a 160-gigabyte MP3 player.

SMALL BUT MIGHTY ▼
More than 200 million people worldwide own an MP3 player. For many, the device offers everything that vinyl records, tape cassettes, and CDs lack: an almost endless choice of songs that they can select from and listen to at any time, anywhere. The formats used in the past—both the recordings and the devices for playing them—took up much more space, were hard to carry, could get scratched or tangled, and didn't allow people to buy individual songs. Musicians and engineers continue to explore even better ways of capturing the sound of live music.

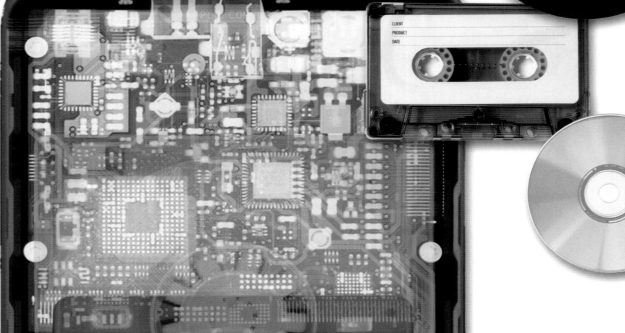

HOW MUCH MUSIC WILL FIT? ▲
Twelve-inch vinyl records typically hold about 26 minutes of music per side, and music cassettes hold about the same. Most commercial CDs can hold 74 minutes of music, taking up about 700 megabytes (MB). If music is compressed into the MP3 format and burned onto a CD, the CD can hold up to 13 hours of music. Some of today's MP3 players can hold more than 2,000 hours of your favorite songs. That means that you could listen to your MP3 player nonstop for more than 83 days without repeating a song!

◄ ELECTRONIC COMPONENTS
Inside each MP3 player is a circuit board with computer chips, a processor, and memory. By pushing a button or touching a screen, an electric circuit is completed and signals are sent to execute commands.

MRI

If you have ever injured yourself playing a sport, you likely had X-rays to see if you broke a bone or tore a ligament. Magnetic resonance imaging (MRI) is also a method doctors employ to record images of the body. Unlike X-rays and CT scans, which rely on radiation, MRI uses a powerful magnet and radio waves to record the body in cross-sectional images. The images are remarkably detailed. MRI helps doctors detect problems in parts of the body that are not easily seen by other imaging methods. An MRI exam allows doctors to identify or diagnose problems and conditions in the brain, spinal cord, circulatory system, eyes, ears, lungs, joints, tendons, ligaments, and cartilage.

PRODUCING MRI IMAGES ▼

An MRI scan produces precise images of body tissue, creating a two-dimensional (2-D) or three-dimensional (3-D) map of the study area. A computer then combines all the data to make a 2-D or 3-D model. The 2-D pictures are called *slices*, which can be displayed on a computer monitor or put on film. One MRI exam can produce hundreds of images.

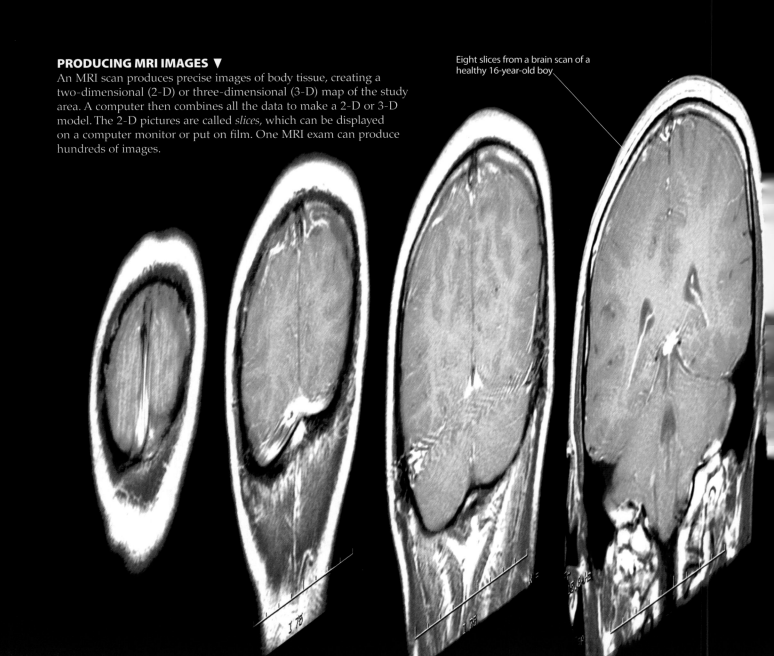

Eight slices from a brain scan of a healthy 16-year-old boy

HOW AN MRI SCANNER WORKS ▶

Patients lie on a table that slides into a long cylinder inside a magnet. When the power is switched on, a magnetic field is strengthened, forcing hydrogen atoms in the body to line up. Radio signals are then sent out by the coils and cause the atoms to spin. Then the coils stop sending radio signals, and the atoms slow down and release their excess energy. This excess energy signal is now received by the coils and sent to the computer. The computer interprets the signals to create the images.

did you know?.....................
THE MRI MAGNET PRODUCES A MAGNETIC FIELD ABOUT 10,000 TIMES GREATER THAN EARTH'S MAGNETIC FIELD.

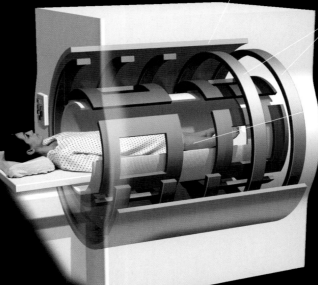

Magnet

Coils

To obtain precise images of the study area, the patient must lie very still inside the MRI machine.

The magnet and coils create a strong magnetic field that surrounds the patient.

Different types of tissue send back different radio waves. This MRI scan produced detailed images of the brain.

Nose

Eyes

The bones and tissues in the facial area look very different from the brain tissue.

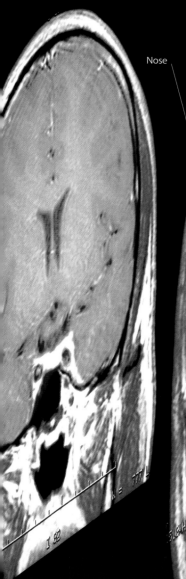

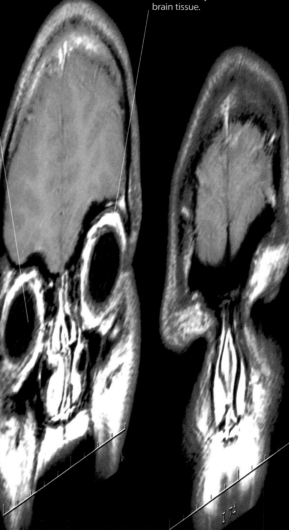

MUTATIONS

Why do some people have brown hair and some people have red hair? The simple answer is genes. Genes, regions of a person's chromosomes, direct cells to produce specific proteins. These proteins help determine the physical traits of a person or any other living thing. But even though cells and cellular processes are pretty amazing, they are not always perfect. Sometimes a change in the DNA of a gene, called a *mutation*, can occur and cause a cell to make an incorrect protein. Since proteins affect an organism's physical traits, mutations in the genes that make these proteins can alter an organism's traits. Red hair, with its accompanying freckles and light-colored skin, is a mutation. So is a genetic disorder such as Type 1 diabetes. Mutations can be helpful, harmful, or neither. Mutations contribute to the astonishing diversity of living things.

◄ FIVE-LEGGED SHEEP

Although it seems rare, there have been cases all over the world of animals born with extra limbs. The mutation of a gene involved in limb development can cause extra limbs to form. Depending on the situation, many of these animals can live happily. This five-legged sheep was born in 2002 in the Netherlands. Her owner said she was able to live with her extra limb without problems. A lamb in New Zealand was born with seven legs. It unfortunately was unable to survive because of other health issues.

WHITE TIGER ►

White tigers can be born when both parents carry a recessive gene for the white color. The majority of white tigers are found in captivity. They are at a disadvantage in the wild and, therefore, are very rare there. Orange and black tigers can hide in the jungle. It's more difficult than you would think to spot a tiger among jungle plants. But a white tiger is much more visible, making hunting without being seen difficult.

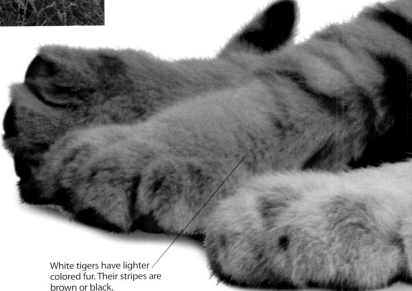

White tigers have lighter colored fur. Their stripes are brown or black.

did you know?
MANY ZOOLOGISTS BELIEVE THAT ALL WHITE TIGERS IN THE UNITED STATES ARE THE DESCENDANTS OF A SINGLE WHITE TIGER.

White tigers usually have blue eyes, while typical tigers have yellow eyes.

BLUE LOBSTER ▲

If you could pick what color lobster you'd like to be, you might want to choose blue. A blue lobster's color is the result of a mutation that causes excess production of a certain protein. These lobsters are rare, and when they're caught, they most often end up in zoos and aquariums instead of a cooking pot. In this case, the mutation is definitely a good thing.

NAMING

Pseudacris triseriata

What's in a name? A lot of information! Scientists name organisms by the characteristics they share, using a system called *binomial nomenclature.* Each organism gets two names—its genus and its species, usually in Latin or Greek. Members of a genus share most characteristics. Each species can reproduce only with another member of its species. These two-part names are an organism's ID. Take this frog, *Pseudacris triseriata,* for example. The genus name, *Pseudacris,* means "false locust," probably because it makes an insectlike sound. Its species name, *triseriata,* means "three-striped." In addition to genus and species, organisms are also grouped into larger levels of classification. For example, *Pseudacris triseriata* and all of the living things shown here are organisms whose cells have a nucleus, so their first level of classification, called *domain,* is Eukarya. This frog's next level, called *kingdom,* is Animalia, followed by its phylum, which is Chordata. The next levels are class (amphibian), order (a frog), and family (a tree frog). Finally, we get down to the levels of genus and species, a false locust with three stripes on its back, commonly called a striped chorus frog.

The genus name *Euglena* comes from two Greek roots that mean "good eye." *Euglena* have an eye spot that helps them sense light.

THE PROTIST AND THE FUNGI

You may have seen a member of the genus *Euglena* when you looked at a drop of pond water through a microscope. The one above is a model of one of more than 200 species in the genus. *Euglena* are in the kingdom Protista, the protists, which are organisms that are neither animal nor plant. *Euglena* are pulled through the water by their tail-like flagella, yet have plantlike structures that enable them to make their own food. Fungi, such as mushrooms, bread mold, and ring worm, have their own kingdom too, because unlike plants, they cannot make their own food.

▼ MEMBERS OF THE PLANT KINGDOM

Organisms in the Plantae kingdom produce their own food through the process of photosynthesis. They range from tiny rootless mosses to giant redwoods. The largest and most diverse phylum in the kingdom is Magnoliophyta, also known as angiosperms or flowering plants. The flowering plants are divided into monocots and dicots according to the type of seed the plant produces.

The classification of seaweeds, which are a type of multicellular algae, is in flux. Some systems place the phylum Rhodophyta, or red algae, in the plant kingdom; others place it in the protist kingdom; and some even say Rhodophyta should form its own kingdom. There are thousands of species of red algae, many of which are edible.

did you know?
A SPECIES OF DINOSAUR DISCOVERED IN 2006 WAS NAMED *DRACOREX HOGWARTSIA,* MEANING DRAGON KING OF HOGWARTS, BECAUSE IT LOOKED LIKE SOMETHING HARRY POTTER MIGHT HAVE MET UP WITH AT HIS SCHOOL FOR WIZARDS.

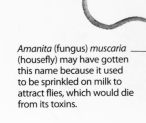

Amanita (fungus) *muscaria* (housefly) may have gotten this name because it used to be sprinkled on milk to attract flies, which would die from its toxins.

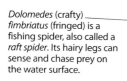

Dolomedes (crafty) *fimbriatus* (fringed) is a fishing spider, also called a *raft spider*. Its hairy legs can sense and chase prey on the water surface.

Members of the *Raja* (ray) genus have angular bodies and sharp tails. *Raja montagui*, or spotted ray, is named for a nineteenth-century British naturalist, George Montagu.

▼ WELCOME TO THE ANIMALIA KINGDOM

Classifying organisms gets more interesting every day, as scientists discover similarities in the genetic material of various organisms. The cells of two similar-looking organisms may also show unexpected differences. The kingdom Animalia has a huge range of organisms with different shapes and parts. Animals in the largest phylum, Arthropoda, have an exoskeleton, or hard outer shell. The spider shown here is from the Arachnida class within that phylum. The three organisms below the spider are in the phylum Chordata, which includes all the vertebrates—animals with backbones—plus animals such as the spotted ray, which has a vertical supporting structure made of cartilage, a softer tissue than bone.

Loxia curvirostra, the common crossbill, is in the finch family. Its two-part name means "slanted curved beak," a feature that enables it to get seeds out of pine cones.

Equus grevyi, Grevy's zebra, is named after Jules Grévy, president of France in the 1880s. One of these animals was sent to him as a gift.

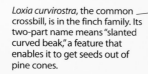

Peas are dicots, with two seed leaves, which is why the pea can be split to make soup. Edible peas are called *Pisum sativa,* meaning sown or useful peas.

Wheat, like most grasses, is a monocot, with one seed leaf. Its name, *Triticum aestivum,* translates roughly as "ripening in summer."

In the early 1800s, astronomers knew of only 7 planets in our solar system. Although Galileo had seen a bright "star" through his telescope in 1613, he didn't realize that it was a planet. In 1845, the French mathematician Urbain Le Verrier realized that the orbit of Uranus—the seventh known planet—was very different from what his calculations predicted it should be. He reasoned that the only way Uranus could move the way it did along its orbit was if another large planet's gravity was pulling on it. In 1846, German astronomer Johann Gottfried Galle used Le Verrier's prediction and found that large planet was Neptune! Neptune is about 4 times as wide as Earth and 17 times more massive.

Planet Neptune is one of the four gas giants in our solar system. Its solid core is about the size of Earth. Surrounding its icy, rocky core is a layer of liquids, including water, and a thick, cloudy atmosphere.

A STORMY SURFACE ▶

Neptune's thick layer of gases and clouds has winds that blow faster than 1,000 miles per hour (about 1,600 km/h). The clouds on the surface are made up of methane—the same gas you burn in a gas stove. Methane gives the planet its blue color. Darker clouds that lie beneath the methane are probably made of hydrogen sulfide—the chemical that gives rotten eggs their yucky smell.

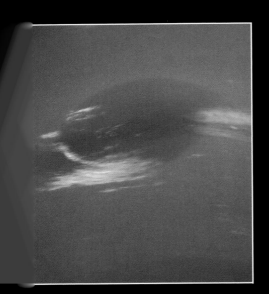

GREAT DARK SPOT ▲

In 1989, an NASA spacecraft named *Voyager 2* took pictures of a dark storm on Neptune's surface. This swirling, hurricane-like storm was almost the size of Earth! Scientists called it the Great Dark Spot. Five years later, it was nowhere to be found, but another huge storm, seen in 1994, lasted 3 years. Imagine what would happen to Earth if a hurricane lasted for 3 years!

Solar System

Mercury   Earth   Jupiter   Saturn   Uranus   Neptune

Venus   Mars

Sun

This chart shows the order of the planets from the sun. Neptune is the eighth planet from the sun.

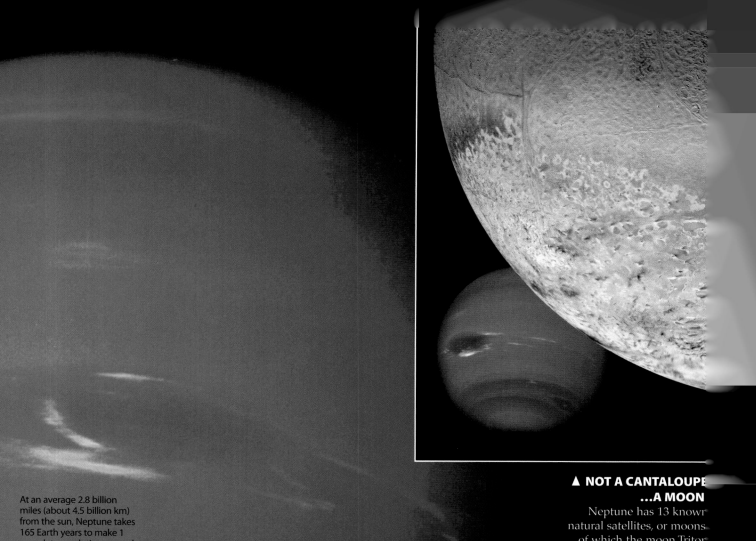

At an average 2.8 billion miles (about 4.5 billion km) from the sun, Neptune takes 165 Earth years to make 1 complete revolution around the sun.

▲ NOT A CANTALOUPE
...A MOON

Neptune has 13 known natural satellites, or moons, of which the moon Triton is the largest. Its surface resembles a cantaloupe and has temperatures of about −400°F (−240°C). Triton is one of the coldest places in the solar system! It is so cold that, instead of lava, volcanoes spew icy mixtures that freeze like snow as they fall back to the ground. Triton also orbits Neptune in the opposite direction of the planet's rotation, leading scientists to believe that this moon was captured by the planet's gravity long after the two had formed.

NEW BODY PARTS

Our bodies can grow new blood cells, hair, nails, and skin. They can repair minor bone injuries and regrow liver tissue. But they cannot regrow entire limbs the way some animals can. We can cut flatworms and sea sponges into pieces, and each piece will grow into a complete animal. More complex animals like crabs and lobsters can regrow claws, eyes, and legs. Regenerating body parts involves unspecialized cells, called *stem cells,* that can grow into any type of cell. Scientists are researching these animals that can regenerate body parts in hopes they can one day duplicate limb regeneration in humans.

did you know?..........................
SCIENTIFIC EVIDENCE SUGGESTS THAT THE POTENTIAL TO REGROW LIMBS IS IN OUR GENES—BUT, FOR NOW, THOSE GENES REMAIN INACTIVE.

SEA STARS ►
Most sea star species can regrow an arm if the central disc (the center of the body) is undamaged. A few species can regrow an entire body from a single arm. Scientists have found a DNA structure (gene) in gray sand star larvae that is similar to one in human embryos. The gene is involved in embryonic development and wound repair. Scientists believe they can use gray sand star larvae as a model to research wound healing and tissue regrowth in humans.

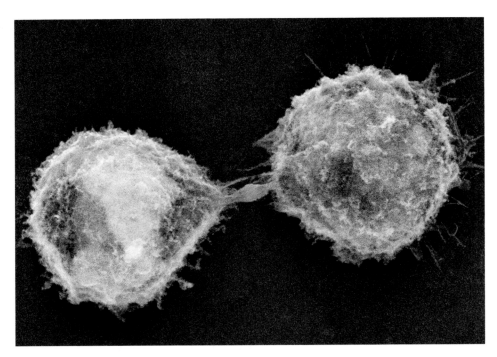

▲ HOW DO BODY PARTS REGENERATE?
Stem cells renew themselves by cell division, giving rise to two identical daughter cells. Then, through a process called *specialization*, they can become any type of cell—skin, muscle, nerve, and other tissues. Specialized cells can revert to stem cells in animals that regenerate body parts. Cell-to-cell communication gives the stem cells instructions, such as what type of cells to become and where they belong.

When a lizard tail breaks off, it separates on a special plane in the middle of a vertebra.

THE LIZARD'S ESCAPE STRATEGY ▲
Many lizard species can voluntarily break off their tails to get away from attacking predators. Afterward, the lizard can regenerate skin, muscle, fat, cartilage, and neural tissues to regrow a new tail. The new tail, however, is not as long or strong as the original as it has a cartilage rod rather than vertebrae.

This sea star is regenerating two arms.

NIAGARA FALLS

Niagara Falls is a true wonder of nature. About 18,000 years ago, during the glacial phase of the last ice age, advancing ice sheets 1–2 miles (about 2–3 km) thick gouged an immense area of land. When the ice melted, the basin was filled with water, forming the North American Great Lakes. The Niagara River connects Lake Erie to Lake Ontario. Niagara Falls has been shaped by erosion from the river's water flowing over a cliff for thousands of years. The water erodes the falls about a foot per year. At this rate, they will retreat all the way back to Lake Erie, a distance of 20 miles (about 32 km) in some 50,000 years. Niagara Falls is the largest and most powerful waterfall in North America and its waters are used to generate electric power.

Water plummets some 188 feet (about 57 m).

HYDROELECTRIC POWER

A concrete and steel dam 1.6 miles (2.6 km) upriver from Niagara Falls controls the amount of water that reaches the falls. At night and during the winter, much of the water that would normally go over Niagara Falls is diverted into underground tunnels. The 45-foot (about 14-m) wide, 5.5-mile (about 9-km) long tunnels carry about 22.5 million gallons (85 million L) of water per minute to hydroelectric plants in Canada and the United States. The plants provide electric power to people in southern Canada and western New York. After the water is used, it is returned to the Niagara River below the falls.

HOW THE FALLS ERODE

The huge amount of water that flows over the falls at high speed causes great erosion of the rock below. The type of erosion that occurs at the base of waterfalls is called *cavitation*. As the water flows over the falls, it becomes filled with thousands of tiny bubbles of water vapor. The pressure of the water on the bubbles causes them to collapse. The burst of energy released by the collapsing bubbles transfers to the rocks. Over time, this bombardment causes the rocks to disintegrate.

▲ BRINK OF THE FALLS

At Niagara Falls, the very hard top layer of riverbed rock, or *caprock*, is dolomite. This caprock is very hard to erode. But the lower layers are softer sedimentary rock, like shale. Shale dissolves in water to form mud or clay. Over time, the rushing water wears away the lower layers of soft rock, creating an overhang of the caprock. Eventually the overhang breaks off and falls into the river below.

The deepest section of the Niagara River is just below the falls, where the water has carved out a hole about as deep as the falls are high.

The water is green from the minerals in dissolved limestone, shale, and sandstone.

did you know?..............

ON AVERAGE, 45 MILLION GALLONS (ABOUT 170 MILLION L) OF WATER FALL OVER THE CREST OF NIAGARA FALLS EVERY MINUTE.

NIGHT VISION GOGGLES

When you walk into a dark room, your eyes take a minute to adjust to the low light and eventually you begin to see the shapes of things. Night vision goggles (NVGs) not only take in low light, but they also intensify the light so that you can see much more than you would be able to see without them. Military personnel, police officers, pilots, and other groups that need to work at night use this technology. The goggles work because of the effect that certain photons—particles of light—have on some materials, such as metals. Photons from certain types of light can give enough energy to the electrons in the metal to knock them out of orbit around their atoms. These electrons flow out of the metal, causing a series of reactions that increases the number of photons that hit your eyes.

HOW IT WORKS ▼

A night vision camera works similarly to the way NVGs work. The camera lens collects light. The light then goes into a tube called an *image intensifier tube*, where several things happen, as shown below. There must be some visible light for these devices to work, usually from stars or from distant city lights shining up into the sky.

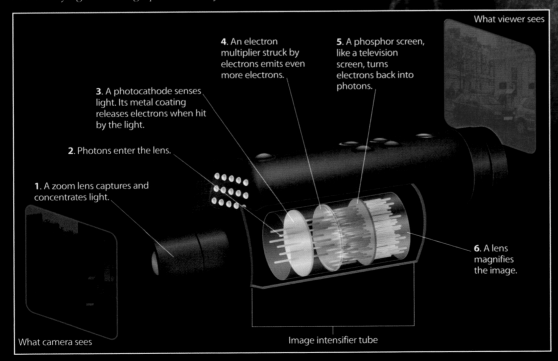

What viewer sees

4. An electron multiplier struck by electrons emits even more electrons.

5. A phosphor screen, like a television screen, turns electrons back into photons.

3. A photocathode senses light. Its metal coating releases electrons when hit by the light.

2. Photons enter the lens.

1. A zoom lens captures and concentrates light.

6. A lens magnifies the image.

What camera sees

Image intensifier tube

▲ WHAT YOU SEE

NVGs can amplify low light thousands of times. The scene usually looks green because NVG phosphor screens are colored green. The human eye can see more shades of green than of any other color produced by a phosphor. The latest generation of NVGs produces a black-and-white image.

Night vision devices have been developed over the last 60 years, with constant improvements. The devices have become smaller and lighter, and provide a much clearer image. Many NVGs can use the infrared portion of the electromagnetic spectrum, in addition to the small amount of visible light available. Infrared light is used for sensing the heat of objects in the field of view.

did you know?
SOME ANIMALS' EYES SHINE BACK AT YOU BECAUSE THEY HAVE A NIGHT-VISION STRUCTURE, CALLED A *TAPETUM*. IT REFLECTS LIGHT, MAKING MORE LIGHT AVAILABLE FOR SENSING.

OH 1×20

When looking into goggles, you are actually looking at the phosphor screen.

NO SMOKING

Bad breath, stinky, stained fingers, unhealthy skin, and a wheezing cough—smokers are hardly the picture of health and beauty. This bad habit that can make people unattractive can also kill them. About 80–90 percent of all lung cancer deaths are the result of smoking. Smoking also leads to heart disease, which is the leading cause of death in the United States. Cigarettes may not kill quickly, but they are highly addictive. Nicotine, the main drug in cigarettes, causes the body to release adrenaline, the chemical that makes you excited when you are surprised or scared. While nicotine might provide a short-lived lift, over time it increases the brain's need for this stimulation. Trying to quit can be very difficult. Strong cravings can cause a person to feel grouchy and hungry, and to have difficulty paying attention and sleeping.

A BOUQUET OF POISONS ▶

You may be surprised to know that nicotine does not cause cancer. However, cigarette smoke contains more than 60 other chemicals that do. Toxins such as formaldehyde, arsenic, vinyl chloride, and benzene are all found in cigarettes. In addition to addictive and cancer-causing substances, smoke contains other poisons. Carbon monoxide, lead, and cyanide are just a few.

TROUBLED BREATHING ▶

This smoker is receiving oxygen therapy for emphysema. Emphysema is a respiratory disease often caused when smoking permanently destroys the walls of the tiny air sacs in lungs. During normal breathing, these air sacs exchange carbon dioxide waste with fresh oxygen. Thus, people with emphysema have trouble getting enough oxygen from air. To make sure they get enough oxygen to breathe, they may carry a tank that delivers oxygen through a mask.

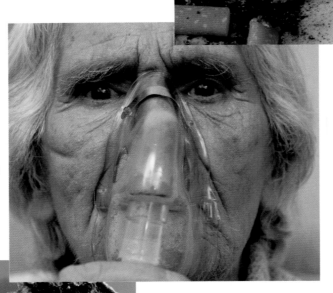

◀ GOOD LUNG, BAD LUNG

It is pretty easy to tell that the stained, deformed lung on the right has been damaged by smoking. Special white blood cells in the air sacs of your lungs, called *alveolar macrophages,* help protect the lungs. They do this by engulfing foreign particles that are inhaled, such as dust or bacteria. Cigarette smoke contains so many impurities that these cells become filled with particles, making smokers' lungs look gray or black. In addition, smokers' air sacs can become inflamed. They release substances that damage the walls of the air sacs. The sacs become scarred, and over time, the scarring makes the lungs less stretchy. Lung tissues that are stiff and inflexible make breathing difficult.

did you know?

ALMOST 1 OUT OF EVERY 5 DEATHS IN THE UNITED STATES IS RELATED TO SMOKING. ABOUT 440,000 AMERICANS DIE EACH YEAR BECAUSE OF TOBACCO.

SAY NO TO EARLY AGING ▶

Smoking cigarettes not only can cause early death, it also speeds up the aging process. Smokers get wrinkles, yellow teeth, and weaker bones more quickly than nonsmokers. Shortness of breath and strain on the heart make it more difficult for smokers to compete with nonsmoking peers in sports. A smoker has a harder time recovering from injuries because smoking slows the body's ability to heal.

NUCLEAR MEDICINE

Radioactivity may signal "Danger!" in your mind. However, a branch of medicine, called *nuclear medicine*, uses radioactivity to help diagnose and treat diseases. Nuclear medicine takes advantage of the fact that radioactive substances are unstable. This means that the isotopes of certain chemical elements emit particles with high-energy values, such as gamma rays. Isotopes are atoms of the same element with different numbers of neutrons. When radioactive drugs are injected into the human body, their particles give off energy that is detected to create images of the areas where they were absorbed. This helps locate problems in the body. The drugs used in this imaging process do not harm the body. However, the gamma rays these drugs emit can be used to destroy cells. For example, harmful cancer cells are often targeted with gamma radiation. Another example is the use of radioactive drugs to treat the thyroid gland—an important gland in your body that helps regulate your metabolism.

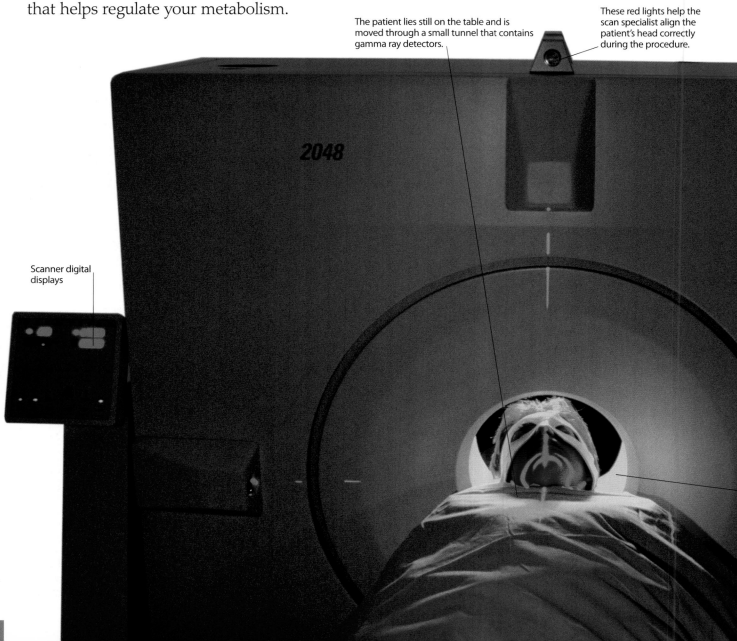

The patient lies still on the table and is moved through a small tunnel that contains gamma ray detectors.

These red lights help the scan specialist align the patient's head correctly during the procedure.

2048

Scanner digital displays

RADIO PHARMACOLOGY ►

This chemist is blending radioactive chemicals to make radiopharmaceuticals. These are drugs that emit radioactivity. They are also called radiotracers, because their emissions can be traced. The glassed-in safety chamber shown here, along with the chemist's special clothing, will protect him from radioactivity as he mixes the chemicals.

Different chemicals are absorbed by different parts of the body. Radioactive nitrogen, for example, is used to trace blood circulation in the heart and lungs.

know? did you
UP TO 12 MILLION NUCLEAR MEDICINE IMAGING AND OTHER PROCEDURES ARE CARRIED OUT EVERY YEAR IN THE UNITED STATES.

◄ PATIENT IN PET SCANNER

This PET doesn't live in a house! PET stands for Positron Emission Tomography. Positrons are positively charged particles that are emitted from some radioactive substances. In a PET scan, a patient receives, usually through an injection, a radioactive drug that is absorbed by certain tissues of the body. As the drug passes through the body, the machine measures the gamma rays that are produced when positrons collide with electrons in the body. The patient is moved through the machine, and a series of images of the body are formed. Doctors analyze the images to look for signs of disease, such as tumors. PET scans are also used to see how organs and tissues, such as your heart and lungs, are functioning.

Crystals in the machine convert gamma rays into light, which is then converted into electrical signals. These go to a computer, which produces the images.

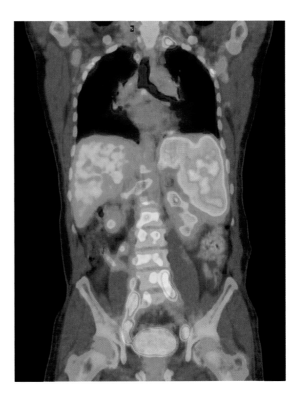

PET SCAN ▲

Patients undergoing a PET scan swallow, inhale, or are injected with a radiotracer material. The scanner detects the radioactive emissions from the injected material that enhances the image for doctors. This PET scan image shows abnormal growths in a patient's abdomen and chest caused by non-Hodgkin's lymphoma, a type of cancer that affects white blood cells. In this case, the PET scan images show doctors how far the cancer cells have developed.

OCEAN CURRENTS

The water in the ocean is in constant motion. It moves in huge continuous streams we call *currents.* When you see waves crashing against the shore, you are looking at the power of ocean currents. But how do they form? Ocean currents are of three basic types: surface currents, deep currents, and tidal currents. They are caused by wind, gravity, and water density, and are also affected by the position of the continents. Surface currents occur in the top 328 feet (100 m) of the ocean and are driven mainly by wind. They have a big impact on Earth's weather and climate. Deep currents sweep along the seafloor and are driven by water density and gravity. Tides, caused by the gravitational pull of the moon and sun, move water up and down. Although tidal currents affect smaller areas than other ocean currents do, they are important because they affect life, transport, and commerce along the coasts.

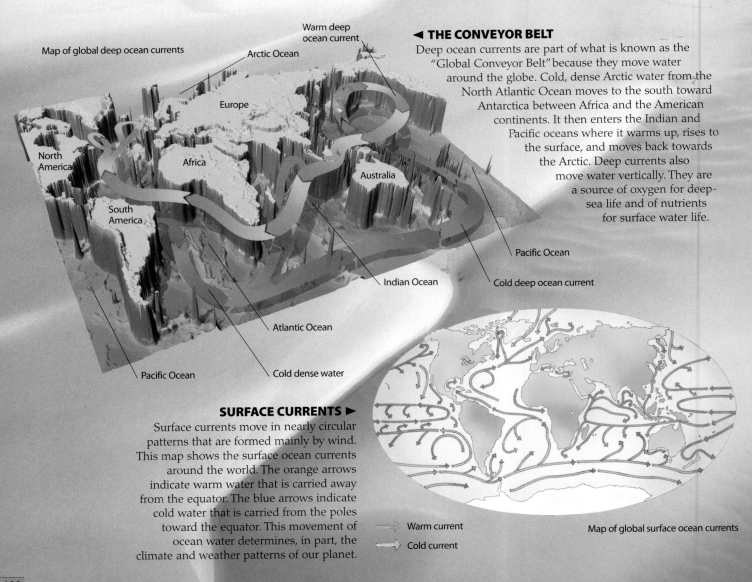

Map of global deep ocean currents

Warm deep ocean current

Arctic Ocean

Europe

Africa

Australia

North America

South America

Pacific Ocean

Indian Ocean

Atlantic Ocean

Pacific Ocean

Cold dense water

Cold deep ocean current

◄ THE CONVEYOR BELT

Deep ocean currents are part of what is known as the "Global Conveyor Belt" because they move water around the globe. Cold, dense Arctic water from the North Atlantic Ocean moves to the south toward Antarctica between Africa and the American continents. It then enters the Indian and Pacific oceans where it warms up, rises to the surface, and moves back towards the Arctic. Deep currents also move water vertically. They are a source of oxygen for deep-sea life and of nutrients for surface water life.

SURFACE CURRENTS ▶

Surface currents move in nearly circular patterns that are formed mainly by wind. This map shows the surface ocean currents around the world. The orange arrows indicate warm water that is carried away from the equator. The blue arrows indicate cold water that is carried from the poles toward the equator. This movement of ocean water determines, in part, the climate and weather patterns of our planet.

Warm current

Cold current

Map of global surface ocean currents

California

Hawaiian Islands

EL NIÑO ▲

El Niño is the periodic irregular warming of water from the coasts of Ecuador and Peru to the central Pacific Ocean. During an El Niño period, the winds become weaker. This allows warm currents to flow from the west, heating the usually colder surface of the ocean. The yellow, orange, and red in this map of the Pacific Ocean indicate the warm waters of El Niño. El Niño is thought to have contributed to some torrential rainfalls in South America and the United States in the last couple of decades, as well as drought in Australia and record high temperatures in Europe.

Rip currents, which carry tidal waters back toward the sea, can be a hazard to swimmers.

TIDES

A tide is an alternating high and low point in sea level with reference to land. Tides are produced mainly by the gravitational pull of the moon, and to a lesser extent by that of the sun. Twice a day, water pushes onto the shore and then flows away in a predictable way. The current produced by a high tide is known as a *flood current*. The current produced by a low tide is called an *ebb current*. Tides can determine when ships can enter port and when or where fishers can expect a better catch. Tides are an essential part of the daily lives of coastal peoples.

Tidal currents and surface currents move sand around, creating dangerous sandbars and deep channels.

Mariners in small boats or large ships must be aware of the power of currents.

OCTOPUS

Although octopuses spend a lot of time lounging or strolling along the ocean floor using the suckers on their arms, they can move fast if they are hunting for food or escaping danger. Octopuses propel themselves by repeatedly taking in and squirting water out of a tube near their eyes, called a *funnel*. This maneuvering requires a well-developed circulatory system. Octopuses are one of the few invertebrates with a closed circulatory system, which means their blood is contained and transported inside the blood vessels. This allows blood, dissolved oxygen, and nutrients to travel quickly through the body. Octopuses power their circulation with three hearts: one large heart that pumps blood to the body and two smaller hearts that pump blood to the gills, which are responsible for respiration.

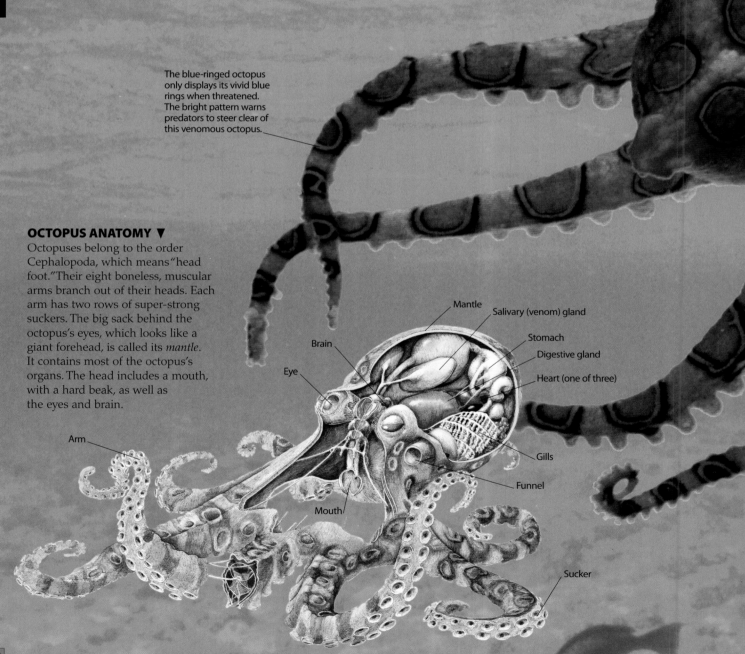

The blue-ringed octopus only displays its vivid blue rings when threatened. The bright pattern warns predators to steer clear of this venomous octopus.

OCTOPUS ANATOMY ▼

Octopuses belong to the order Cephalopoda, which means "head foot." Their eight boneless, muscular arms branch out of their heads. Each arm has two rows of super-strong suckers. The big sack behind the octopus's eyes, which looks like a giant forehead, is called its *mantle*. It contains most of the octopus's organs. The head includes a mouth, with a hard beak, as well as the eyes and brain.

Mantle

Salivary (venom) gland

Brain

Stomach

Digestive gland

Eye

Heart (one of three)

Arm

Gills

Funnel

Mouth

Sucker

◄ BLUE-RINGED OCTOPUS

Blue-ringed octopuses, which live off the Australian coast, produce highly toxic venom for which no known antidote exists. In just minutes, the venom can kill an adult human! The toxin is produced by bacteria that live in the octopus's salivary glands. Despite their deadly venom, blue-ringed octopuses are shy creatures that weigh less than a golf ball. They are only aggressive toward humans when provoked.

OCTOPUS CAMOUFLAGE ▼

Octopuses are nature's quick-change artists. In the blink of an eye, they can change their skin's color, pattern, and texture by triggering color-changing pigment cells in their skin, called *chromatophores*. Octopuses use this ability to blend into their environment or to startle would-be attackers. When in danger, octopuses will also shoot ink from an ink gland, giving them time to escape.

did you know?..............

OCTOPUSES ARE THOUGHT TO BE THE SMARTEST INVERTEBRATES. IN CAPTIVITY, THEY HAVE BEEN TAUGHT TO UNSCREW THE LID ON A JAR OF SHRIMP.

OIL SPILLS

When you look out your window on a rainy day, it seems as if all the water in the world is coming down at once! Actually, it's only a fraction of all the water on our planet. Water is essential for life on Earth, and 97 percent of it is salty ocean water. Only 3 percent is fresh water, and about a third of that is frozen in the polar ice caps and glaciers. It is our most precious natural resource and yet it is threatened by pollution every day. Water pollution comes in many forms, but one of the worst is from oil spills. Oil is carried across oceans, lakes, and rivers in huge oil tankers. These massive ships can hold more than 50 million gallons (more than 189 million L) of oil. They can run aground, collide with other ships, and even sink, sometimes spilling thousands or millions of gallons of oil into the water, harming the natural environment.

Oiled water birds can't fly and can't float well.

THE DELICATE GREBE ►

A grebe is a water bird that spends most of the year in marine waters along coasts. Grebes dive to catch fish and are great swimmers. But in the event of an oil spill, they are very vulnerable. It's very hard to save a bird once it's been oiled. After the *Exxon Valdez* oil spill, the carcasses of 35,000 water birds were found. Naturalists think as many as 250,000 may have died.

THE BIG SPILL ▲

The oil tanker *Exxon Valdez* ran aground on March 29, 1989, in Prince William Sound, Alaska, spilling almost 11 million gallons (about 41.5 million L) of crude oil into the ocean. It is considered to be the largest oil spill in U.S. history, causing great damage to the environment. Approximately 1,300 miles (about 2,092 km) of shoreline were affected. The spill killed thousands of birds; millions of fish; hundreds of seals, sea otters, and bald eagles; and at least 22 killer whales.

Oil and water don't mix, but oil spreads very fast and can pollute thousands of miles of seashore.

did you know?
VOLUNTEERS AND VETERINARIANS USED DISHWASHING

Boom

Oil can blind
a bird. A blind animal
cannot hunt for food or
protect itself from predators.

Oil on the feathers of birds
destroys their natural
insulation. Birds that can't
maintain normal body heat
will die.

CLEANING UP ▲

Cleaning an oil spill is tricky. Oil can be partially contained with a
floating barrier called a *boom*, which has a skirt that goes below the
water surface. The oil can then be skimmed off the surface, or large
sponges, called *sorbents*, can soak up the oil. But if the sea gets rough,
the spill can break up, making it very hard to clean. High-pressure water
can be used to wash oil away from beaches and trap it so it can be
removed. In other places, the oil is left to biodegrade.

Cleanup workers wear
protective clothing to avoid
coming into contact with oil
and other pollutants.

OPEN-HEART SURGERY

The heart is essential to the human body. Without it, blood would not move and could not deliver materials to cells, remove wastes, or fight disease. If a heart isn't working properly, it needs to be fixed. Today, surgeons can fix many heart ailments with open-heart surgery. It's called open-heart surgery because the chest is opened to reach the heart. In 2006 in the United States, surgeons performed 694,000 open-heart surgeries. Bypass surgeries, in which blocked arteries are bypassed using a vessel from elsewhere in the body, accounted for most of the surgeries. Valve replacements ranked number two, and 2,210 of the total surgeries were heart transplants. Technologies such as heart-lung machines, minimally invasive procedures, and robotic assistance enable heart surgeons to save many lives that could not have been saved previously. New procedures are changing the definition of open-heart surgery.

A NEW VALVE ▶

Human heart valves are like doors that open in one direction to let blood through, but do not let it flow back. Although a heart has four valves, the two on the left side of the heart control the flow of blood to most of the body. They work harder, so they are much more likely to need repair or replacement. Valve replacements can be mechanical (made of plastic, carbon, or metal) or biological (made of animal tissue). Sometimes a patient's own tissue can even be used to replace a valve.

OPEN HEART = OPEN CHEST ▼

A human heart is well protected by the ribs and sternum. To get to the heart, a surgeon cuts through the sternum and spreads the ribs. At the end of surgery, the sternum is closed and held in place with stainless steel wires or bands.

A DETOUR ▲

During open-heart surgery, the heart is usually not beating, but blood still needs to circulate. A heart-lung machine, also called a cardiopulmonary (heart and lung) bypass machine, can take over the work of the heart and lungs for several hours. It carries blood from the heart to an oxygenator and then carries oxygen-rich blood back to the aorta so it can circulate through the body.

A rib spreader is inserted into the incision in the sternum and slowly opened to separate the ribs, making room for a surgeon to work.

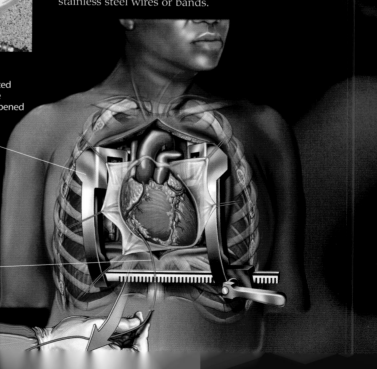

A catheter is placed in the chest cavity to drain fluids and blood after surgery.

did you know?.....................
NEW TECHNIQUES ALLOW SURGEONS TO PERFORM SOME OPERATIONS WITHOUT A HEART-LUNG MACHINE WHILE THE PATIENT'S HEART BEATS

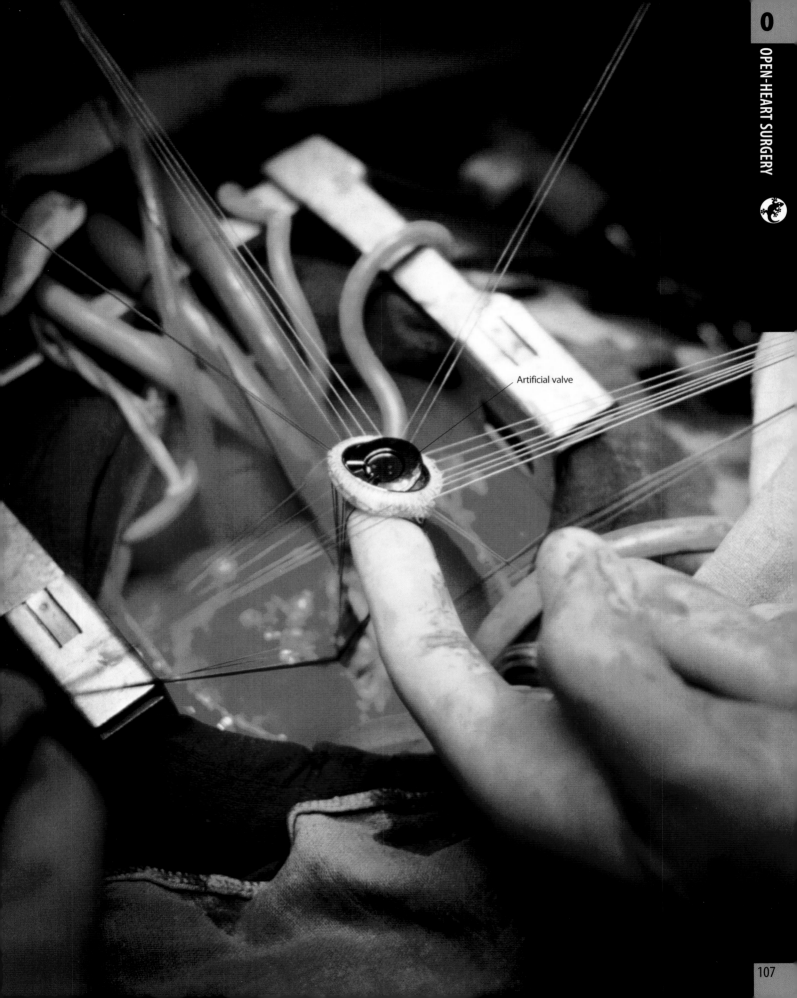

Artificial valve

PANDEMIC

Pathogens—bacteria, viruses, fungi, and protists—cause infectious diseases. These diseases are spread in different ways: through water, food, or soil; via animals; or by human contact. An epidemic occurs when an infectious disease spreads quickly to many people throughout a country or region. An epidemic that spreads rapidly to even more people in different parts of the world is called a *pandemic*. Some diseases that have historically become pandemics are influenza (flu), cholera, and plague. These and other infectious diseases can spread throughout the world more quickly than ever before, due to great increases in international travel. The World Health Organization (WHO) keeps track of infectious diseases around the world and decides when they reach epidemic and pandemic levels. WHO has devised a pandemic preparedness plan that outlines steps that should be taken in the event of an influenza pandemic.

◄ CHOLERA
The pathogen that causes cholera in humans is a type of bacteria. The bacteria enter the intestine when a person drinks contaminated water or eats contaminated food. In severe cases, cholera causes vomiting and diarrhea and, left untreated, can lead to death. In the United States, cholera is not a concern because of the advanced water treatment systems.

Cholera is often associated with watery diarrhea. The bacteria actually produce a cholera toxin that causes this symptom.

◄ IS THE WATER CLEAN?
Some pathogens, such as the bacteria that cause cholera, can live in water. When a healthy person drinks contaminated water, he or she ingests these pathogens and can become ill. Microorganisms can be introduced into groundwater in various ways. For example, fecal contamination from sick animals can seep into groundwater. A leak in a wastewater system can also contaminate water with pathogens. Areas of the world with poor water treatment systems often spur the growth of pandemics because the pathogens may infect great numbers of people in a short time.

In Afghanistan, conflict and drought have affected the cleanliness of the water supply.

NOVEL H1N1 VIRUS ▶

Novel, meaning new, is the best description for this virus that was first seen in humans in the spring of 2009. On June 11, 2009, the World Health Organization officially declared it a pandemic. H1N1 spreads quickly between humans in the same way other flu viruses do—through coughing and sneezing. As opposed to typical flu viruses, H1N1 is harder on people younger than 25 years old than it is on the elderly. Vaccines against H1N1 have been developed.

Inside the H1N1 virus particle is ribonucleic acid, or RNA, which carries the genetic material of the virus.

The outside of the virus is surrounded by a lipid, or fat, envelope.

The spikes are proteins, which scientists use to identify the type of virus.

THE BIRD FLU ▼

Viruses affect different animal populations differently. Avian influenza, commonly known as bird flu, naturally exists in wild bird populations but does not usually make them sick. But bird flu is very contagious between birds. It can be passed to domesticated birds such as chickens and turkeys through saliva, nasal secretions, and feces. In these birds, the virus has caused millions of deaths. Bird flu has crossed over to humans mostly in cases where people have had contact with bodily fluids of infected birds. As with all new viruses, scientists work to develop vaccines. Bird flu vaccines are now being given to domestic bird populations to try to stop the spread of the disease.

did you know?......................................
THERE HAVE BEEN AT LEAST SEVEN CHOLERA PANDEMICS SINCE THE EARLY NINETEENTH CENTURY.

PATTERNS IN NATURE

Patterns are one of nature's adaptations for survival. Take stripes, for example. A tiger's stripes camouflage it in tall grass. A skunk's stripes may warn off predators. A harmless snake's red, black, and yellow stripes may mimic those of the poisonous coral snake. Symmetry is another type of pattern. Sea stars and jellyfish have radial symmetry, as a pie does. This shape lets organisms whose food floats around them sense it from any direction. Organisms that need to move around to find their food are typically bilaterally symmetrical— two halves that are mirror images—and have most of their sensory organs in their head. They can sense danger with their heads and coordinate balanced and fast movement. Certain patterns in nature can even be described mathematically by a sequence of numbers called *Fibonacci numbers*. The number of petals on some flowers, the number of spirals on a pine cone, and some say even the proportions of the human body can be found in this pattern of numbers.

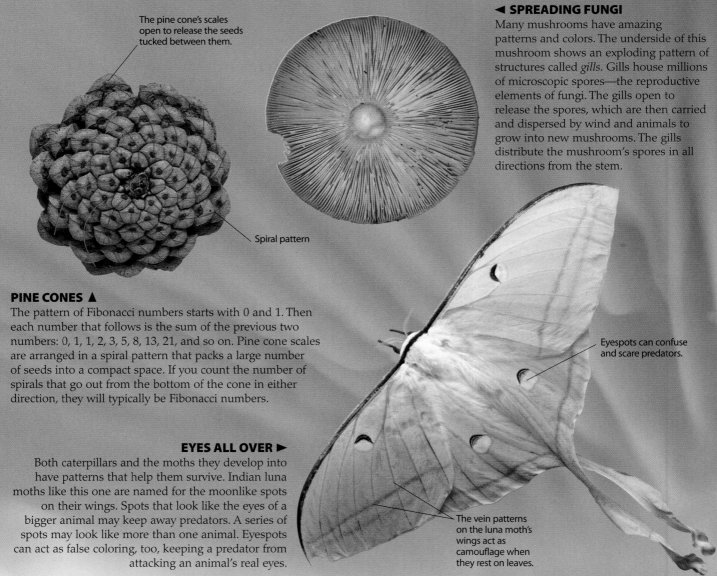

The pine cone's scales open to release the seeds tucked between them.

Spiral pattern

◄ SPREADING FUNGI
Many mushrooms have amazing patterns and colors. The underside of this mushroom shows an exploding pattern of structures called *gills*. Gills house millions of microscopic spores—the reproductive elements of fungi. The gills open to release the spores, which are then carried and dispersed by wind and animals to grow into new mushrooms. The gills distribute the mushroom's spores in all directions from the stem.

PINE CONES ▲
The pattern of Fibonacci numbers starts with 0 and 1. Then each number that follows is the sum of the previous two numbers: 0, 1, 1, 2, 3, 5, 8, 13, 21, and so on. Pine cone scales are arranged in a spiral pattern that packs a large number of seeds into a compact space. If you count the number of spirals that go out from the bottom of the cone in either direction, they will typically be Fibonacci numbers.

Eyespots can confuse and scare predators.

EYES ALL OVER ▶
Both caterpillars and the moths they develop into have patterns that help them survive. Indian luna moths like this one are named for the moonlike spots on their wings. Spots that look like the eyes of a bigger animal may keep away predators. A series of spots may look like more than one animal. Eyespots can act as false coloring, too, keeping a predator from attacking an animal's real eyes.

The vein patterns on the luna moth's wings act as camouflage when they rest on leaves.

◄ FIERCE FACE

The puss moth is a soft, fuzzy creature like the cat it is named after. But the caterpillar that the moth grows from is not! The caterpillar's green and brown segmented body pattern blends with the leaves. When it is disturbed, the caterpillar withdraws its head into the first segment of its body and lifts the round red edge of the segment to face the threat. Two black spots on the red ring look like eyes. This adaptation mimics an animal with a big, fierce face.

Holes the caterpillar breathes through, called *spiracles*, create a pattern, too.

If the mean face doesn't work, the double tail can squirt nasty acid.

did you know?.....................

GEESE FLY IN A "V" PATTERN TO SAVE ENERGY, BY REDUCING WIND RESISTANCE, AND TO KEEP TRACK OF THE OTHER GEESE IN THE FLOCK.

A cross-section cut reveals the beautiful pattern of chambers hidden inside a nautilus shell.

NAUTILUS SHELL ►

The pearly nautilus is a cephalopod, an ancient group that includes octopuses. Nautiluses build their shells as they grow, making each chamber slightly larger than the one before it. Nautiluses use these chambers to regulate the amount of gases and water needed to keep them afloat and upright. The animal lives in the outermost chamber of a spiral.

As it grows, the nautilus seals off the cramped rear part of its living quarters and extends the front edge.

PENGUINS

Penguins are flightless aquatic birds found on every continent in the Southern Hemisphere. There are 18 species of penguins, some of which live on Antarctica. Others live in temperate climates in South Africa, Chile, Australia, and New Zealand. Some species, such as the Galapagos penguin, live in a tropical climate! Penguins are carnivores and eat crabs, squid, fish, and krill. Penguins are also devoted parents. In most species, both parents care for the young and take turns incubating, or warming, the egg so one of them can feed in the sea. When a penguin parent returns to shore after feeding, it has to find its mate and chick. To do so, it vocalizes, or calls out, as it moves through the penguin colony. Its mate and chick can recognize the parent's voice, even while hundreds or thousands of other birds are vocalizing!

did you know?
....
MOST PENGUINS HAVE SPECIAL GLANDS THAT ALLOW THEM TO DRINK SALT WATER.

▼ KING PENGUINS

King penguins are about 3 feet (95 cm) tall, making them the second largest penguins after emperor penguins. Like emperor penguins, kings have a peculiar way of incubating their single egg. Instead of building nests and sitting on their egg as other penguins do, king penguins carry their egg on their feet beneath a fold of skin called a *brood patch.*

ROCKHOPPER PENGUINS ▼

Rockhoppers are small penguins with big attitudes! They stand only about 20 inches (52 cm) tall but are highly aggressive and will peck fearlessly at intruders, including humans. To raise their young, rockhoppers build nests of pebbles and grass along rocky coastlines, often at the top of steep cliffs. To get to their nests, rockhoppers rocket out of the water at high speeds and grab the sides of the cliffs with their sharp nails. They claw their way up the cliffs using their feet and beaks until they reach their nests.

Northern rockhoppers have long, bright yellow crest feathers, red eyes, and blunt, red-brown beaks.

Penguins have lost the ability to fly. Instead, their sturdy wings are well adapted for life in the water.

In addition to waddling, rockhoppers move around by jumping from rock to rock, hence their name.

King penguins will often slide across the ice and snow on their bellies. Scientists call this *tobogganing.*

To stay warm and safe, some penguin chicks huddle together in groups called *crèches*.

PENGUIN CHICKS ▲

Penguin babies are called *chicks*. Most newly hatched chicks are covered in a coat of fine down feathers that are not waterproof. The chicks depend on their parents for food until they get their waterproof juvenile feathers. At that time, they can enter the sea and hunt for themselves.

EMPEROR PENGUINS ▶

The male emperor penguin, standing almost 4 feet (about 115 cm) tall, incubates the egg all by himself while the female feeds at sea. It's a tough job. The male has to balance the egg on his feet, keep it warm, and go without food for about 65 days while the egg incubates. And he has to do it all in the brutal cold of an Antarctic winter! While the chick is still small, it can get back in the brood patch to stay warm.

WATER WORLD

Penguins are a bit awkward on land but are wonders in the water! They use their paddlelike wings, and streamlined body to propel themselves gracefully beneath the waves. Penguins are also fantastic divers. When hunting for fish, king penguins may dive more than 984 feet (300 m) deep. To catch their breath while being pursued by predators, penguins shoot in and out of the water at high speeds, a behavior called *porpoising*.

Penguins use their webbed feet and wedge-shaped tail as a rudder to steer themselves as they slice through the sea.

Like many sea creatures, penguins are *countershaded*—dark on top and light below. Countershading helps camouflage the penguins from predators and their prey.

Penguins have waterproof feathers that overlap and are densely packed to keep water from getting to the skin.

113

PLANT INVASION

An alien invasion is happening—and it could be happening right in your yard. The word *alien* does not apply only to beings from outer space. An alien is anything that comes from another place, such as a foreign land. Species of plants or animals from other ecosystems are aliens. Another name for an alien species is an exotic. An exotic species is an organism that is carried into a new location by people. When people move to a new country, they sometimes bring exotic plants for crops or decoration. Usually exotic species do not do well in their new homes without constant care. Occasionally, however, an exotic species is introduced to the wild and is able to survive. If it can survive, it could harm or even displace native species that live there naturally. Such a takeover by an exotic is called an *invasion*.

COCONUTS INVADE BY SEA ▶
Coconut palm trees live near the shore in the tropics. When the fruits (coconuts) are ripe, they fall from the tree onto the beach. Waves may take the fruits out to sea, where ocean currents carry them to distant beaches. When they arrive on dry land, they can sprout and grow into palm trees. Because people like to eat coconuts, the plant also spreads when people take them from one place to another as food.

VINES TAKE OVER ▶

The mile-a-minute is a fast-growing vine that grows throughout the eastern United States. Its seeds were among holly seeds sent from Japan to a Pennsylvania nursery in the 1930s. The seeds were accidentally planted, and the vine spread throughout its perfect new habitat. Birds and ants disperse the seeds, and water carries seed-bearing fruits that float for days. The vines cover native plants, limiting their exposure to sunlight.

did you know?....................................
IT MAY NOT GROW A MILE A MINUTE, BUT THE MILE-A-MINUTE WEED DOES GROW UP TO 6 INCHES (15.24 CM) A DAY.

DOGS ON PATROL ▶

Some people knowingly or unknowingly carry invasive plants in their travel bags. Rather than go through every bag by hand, airport security often uses sniffer dogs. Sniffer dogs, or detection dogs, are trained to recognize the smell of certain plants. When their keen noses sniff out a telltale odor, these pups let their handlers know which bag might contain the exotic plant.

DK EDUCATION

Design Miranda Brown and Ali Scrivens, The Book Makers
Managing Art Editor Richard Czapnik
Design Director Stuart Jackman
Publisher Sophie Mitchell

PEARSON

The people who made up the *DK Big Ideas of Science Reference Library* team—representing digital product development, editorial, editorial services, manufacturing, and production—are listed below.

Johanna Burke, Jessica Chase, Arthur Ciccone, Amanda Ferguson, Kathryn Fobert, Christian Henry, Sharon Inglis, Russ Lappa, Dotti Marshall, Robyn Matzke, Tim McDonald, Maria Milczarek, Célio Pedrosa, Stephanie Rogers, Logan Schmidt, Christine Whitney

CREDITS

The publisher would like to thank the following for their kind permission to reproduce their photographs:

Key: t-top; b-below/bottom; c-center; l-left; r-right; f-far

Cover and i) Corbis: Micro Discovery (weevil); Alamy Images: MicroScan/Phototake (lettering). **ii–iii)** Getty Images: Chad Ehlers. **iv-v)** NASA: Shuttle crew STS-64. **vi)** Dorling Kindersley: Royal British Columbia Museum, Victoria, Canada. **vii)** Corbis: Jim Reed (b); NASA: ESA/The Hubble Heritage Team/STScI/AURA (tr). **viii)** Science Photo Library: Pasieka. **x–xi)** NASA. **xii)** Getty Images: Tony Graham (bl). **xii–1** Corbis: Jason Lee/Reuters (c). **2** Corbis: Ted Soqui (bl); Dorling Kindersley: Natural History Museum, London (bc). **2–3** Corbis: Momatiuk-Eastcott. **3** Dorling Kindersley: Natural History Museum, London (tl); Science Photo Library (cr). **4** Corbis: Michael Freeman (cl); Getty Images: Sven Nackstrand/AFP (bl). **4–5** Getty Images: Chad Ehlers. **5** Corbis: Steven Kazlowski/Science Faction (tl). **9** Getty Images: Visuals Unlimited/Brandon Cole. **10** NASA (bl). **10–11** NASA: STS-114 Crew. **11** NASA (br). **12–13** Corbis: Bob Krist. **13** Corbis (tr); Arctic-Images (br); Nik Wheeler (cr). **14–15** Corbis: Bob Krist. **16** Corbis: David Bebber/Reuters (l); NASA (cr). **17** NASA: Shuttle crew STS-64. **18** NASA: DLR (c). **19** NASA: JPL/University of Arizona (c); Lunar and Planetary Laboratory (t). **20–21** Corbis: Vittoriano Rastelli (c). **22–23** Corbis: Michael T. Sedam (c). **23** Corbis: Frans Lanting (br). **24** Corbis: Pedro Costa/EPA (c1). **24–25** Corbis: HO/Reuters. **25** NASA: Earth Observatory (tl). **26** Science Photo Library: Will & Deni McIntyre (cl). **26–27** Getty Images: Stephen Jaffe/AFP. **27** Science Photo Library: Pascal Goetgheluck (tr). **29** Science Photo Library: Stephen and Donna O'Meara (tr). **30** Corbis: Wolfgang Flamisch (bl). **32** Bert Hickman/www.capturedlightning.com. **32–33** Bert Hickman/www.capturedlightning.com. **34** Getty Images: Liu Jin/AFP (bl); Science Photo Library: Martin Bond (b). **35** Dorling Kindersley: Science Museum, London (br). **35** Science Photo Library: Alex Bartel (t). **36** NASA: Goddard Space Flight Center Scientific Visualization Studio (b). **37** Dorling Kindersley: Science Museum, London (tr). **38–39** Corbis: Jean Guichard. **39** Dorling Kindersley: Science Museum, London (r). **40** Dorling Kindersley: Natural History Museum, London (cfr). **40–41** Corbis: Jeremy Horner. **42** Corbis: Scott Smith (cl). **42–43** Corbis: Jay Dickman. **45** Corbis: Toussaint Kluiters/EPA (bl). **45** Getty Images: Nicholas Kamm/AFP (cr). **46** Getty Images: Stephen Dunn (l). **46–47** Getty Images: Sebastian D'Souza/AFP. **47** Getty Images: Vince Bucci/AFP (tr). **48–49** Corbis: WildCountry/David Paterson. **49** Corbis: Arte & Immagini srl. **50** NASA: Lunar and Planetary Laboratory (bl). **50–51** NASA. **51** NASA: JPL/Malin Space Science Systems (br, tr). **52** NASA: JPL (cl). **52–53** NASA: JPL/Cornell University. **53** NASA: JPL/Cornell University/OSU (t). **56** Corbis: Tim Graham/Sygma (bl). **57** Corbis: NASA/Roger Ressmeyer (tr); Science Photo Library: Royal Greenwich Observatory (b). **59** Dorling Kindersley: Ironbridge Gorge Museum, Telford, Shropshire. **60–61** Corbis: Simon Jarratt. **62** NASA: Lunar and Planetary Laboratory (b). **62–63** NASA: Mariner 10 Astrogeology Team, U.S. Geological Survey. **63** NASA: Brian Handy/Trace Project (b); Johns Hopkins University Applied Physics Laboratory (t). **64** Science Photo Library: Jean-Claude Revy/A. Carion/ISM (bl). **64–65** Corbis: Charles & Josette Lenars/Comet. **65** Science Photo Library: Jerry Lodriguss (tr); Jean-Claude Revy/A. Carion/ISM (br). **66** Science Photo Library: Dr. Kari Lounatmaa (cl). **66–67** Corbis: Micro Discovery. **67** Science Photo Library: Pascal Goetgheluck (tr). **68** National Geophysical Data Center (c); Science Photo Library: Gary Hincks (br). **68–69** Corbis: Ralph A. Clevenger. **70** NASA: ESA/Hubble Collaboration (cl); STScI/AURA/Hubble Heritage (bl). **70–71** NASA: AURA/Hubble Heritage Team. **71** NASA: Larry Landolfi (tr). **72–73** Getty Images: Stone/Pete Turner. **73** Getty Images: Jon Van De Grift/Visuals Unlimited, Inc. (tr). **74** Getty Images: Ethan Miller (c). **76** NASA (bc). **76–77** NASA. **77** NASA (t). **78** Corbis: DLILLC (br). **78–79** Getty Images: National Geographic/Michael Lewis. **79** Corbis: Robert Holmes (tr). **80–81** Dorling Kindersley: Apple. **82–83** Science Photo Library: Erich Schrempp. **84** Getty Images: Michel Porro (cl). **85** Corbis: Visuals Unlimited (tl). **88** NASA: JPL (cl); Lunar and Planetary Laboratory (b). **88–89** NASA. **89** NASA: JPL (tr). **90** Science Photo Library (cl). **92** Corbis: Bryan F. Peterson/Flirt (b). **94** Science Photo Library (cr). **96** Science Photo Library: Alex Bartel (c); A. Glauberman (bl). **97** Getty Images: Jamie Grill. **98–99** Science Photo Library: Hank Morgan. **99** Science Photo Library: ISM (br); Mason Morfit/Peter Arnold Inc. (t). **100–101** Corbis: George Steinmetz. **101** NASA: Goddard Space Flight Center Scientific Visualization Studio (t). **102–103** Dorling Kindersley: Weymouth Sealife Center. **104** Corbis: Natalie Fobes/Science Faction. **104–105** Corbis: Jim Zuckerman. **105** Corbis: Vince Streano (tr). **106** Getty Images: Nucleus Medical Art, Inc. (br); Science Photo Library: AJ Photo (cl). **106–107** Corbis: Marc Garanger (c). **108** Corbis: Dennis Kunkel Microscopy, Inc./Visuals Unlimited (cl); Farahnaz Karimy/EPA (bl). **109** Science Photo Library: Pasieka (tr); RIA Novosti (b). **114–115** Corbis: Shigeyuki Uenishi/Amanaimages. **115** Corbis: Alistair Baker/Zefa (t); Getty Images: Joel Robine/AFP (b).

All other images © Dorling Kindersley
For further information see: www.dkimages.com